# WELCOME TO

## GOLF LEGENDS

Lunar Press is an independent publishing company that cares greatly about the accuracy of its content.

If you notice any inaccuracies or have anything that you would like to discuss, then please email us at lunarpresspublishers@gmail.com.

Enjoy!

# IF YOU ENJOY THIS BOOK, CHECK OUT...

**Dive deeper** into the Golf Legends universe with
*The Giant Golf Quiz Book!*

With **444 challenging trivia questions** across **15 themed rounds** of varying difficulty, there will be something for everyone!

Complete the set with the **must-have companion book** - perfect for any golf fan.

# CONTENTS

# ABBREVIATIONS
## AND EXTRA GOLF INFORMATION

**Augusta National Golf Club** - The golf course where the Masters has been played every year since it first started in 1934.

**Champions Tour** - The top men's professional golf tour for players aged 50 and over.

**LPGA Tour** - Ladies Professional Golf Association. This was formed in 1950 and is the top professional golf tour for female players around the world.

**NCAA** - National Collegiate Athletic Association. It is the top annual competition in US college golf.

**PGA Tour** - Professional Golfers' Association. It is an American organisation that was formed in 1968 and runs a series of professional men's golf tournaments for the best players in the world.

**Vardon Trophy** - Trophy given to the player with the lowest scoring average on the PGA Tour for the year.

**Vare Trophy** - Trophy given to the player with the lowest scoring average on the LPGA Tour for the year.

# WARM UP

There have been so many incredible players in the history of golf that it would be impossible to include them all in this book. So, we have created a list of who we believe to be the 20 greatest PGA and LPGA Tour players in history to leave the hard part of deciding up to you!

Sure, you can just look at the numbers and see who has won the most **majors** or who has won the most PGA or LPGA Tour titles, but there is so much more that goes into being an all-time golf legend. You need to consider the rivals they faced, the era they played in, the impact they had on golf and so much more. That's the beautiful thing about creating a list like this: it's your own personal opinion that matters! Everyone's will be slightly different and that's the way it should be.

Golf is one of the most competitive and unique sports worldwide, with roughly 80 million people playing regularly and 450 million fans tuning in each year to watch the best players, and for good reason. Every round of golf is completely different and each course brings new challenges. Some favour the big hitters who can bomb their drives 350 yards, some favour the shorter more accurate players who consistently deliver pinpoint irons onto small greens, and some favour players who play with either a **fade** or a **draw**.

Not only is each round unique, but so is every player - we will see a whole range of styles and techniques across these 20 legends! You have the near-flawless swing of Mickey Wright who could smash down 300-yard drives with ease, the incredible accuracy of Byron Nelson who once didn't leave a fairway for an entire tournament and the unique swing of Arnold Palmer, that may have looked strange to those watching, but worked perfectly for him.

In these pages, you will learn about some of the oldest legends in golf who helped shape the sport into what it is today, as well as some current players who are still making history as we speak. We will cover the incredible career of Bobby Jones, who was born over 120 years ago and was the first player in history to win the Grand Slam. No golf list would be complete without Babe Didrikson Zaharias, who was not only the most feared golfer on the planet, but also a two-time Olympic gold medalist in athletics. Some of these stories may seem unbelievable and will read like fiction, but I can assure you that they are completely true.

We will also learn about the history of golf and how it became the game it is today. We'll learn about three women who were the original founders of the LPGA Tour and served as its first presidents, about the player who helped design Augusta National Golf Club and set up the very first Masters, and about the player who invented the modern sand wedge. All of these legends have been intertwined in the incredible history of this sport and have had big parts to play.

Some of the players are still alive today and continue

to work for charitable causes, play on the Champions Tour or run their own golf academies to pave the way for the next generation. Others have passed away, yet their legacies continue to shine as brightly as they did when they were superstars in the golf world. A few are currently playing and their legacies are still being written.

All are legends in their own right, whose stories will live on forever in the history of golf.

# TIGER WOODS

## MAJORS

THE OPEN
CHAMPIONSHIP
X3

PGA
CHAMPIONSHIP
X4

US OPEN
X3

THE MASTERS
X5

TOTAL MAJORS
15

## CAREER STATS

| | |
|---|---|
| WEEKS AT NO. 1 | 683 |
| PGA TOUR WINS | 82 |
| EUROPEAN TOUR WINS | 41 |
| RYDER CUP RECORD | 13-21-3 |
| PGA PLAYER OF THE YEAR | 11 |
| THE PLAYERS CHAMPIONSHIP | 2 |

| PGA WIN % | PRIZE MONEY |
|---|---|
| 82/373 (22%) | $120,954,766 |

Ryder Cup record is in the format of wins-losses-halves

| BORN | DECEMBER 30, 1975 |
|---|---|
| NATIONALITY | AMERICAN |
| TURNED PRO | 1996 |
| HEIGHT | 1.85 M (6 FT 1 IN) |
| PLAYS | RIGHT-HANDED |

# BIOGRAPHY

Although this list of the greatest golfers of all time is in no particular order, there is no one else that we could start with than the one and only Tiger Woods.

Tiger is tied for the most PGA Tour wins, sits second for the most majors won of all time (15) and has been at the heart of so many of golf's most iconic moments throughout history. Every golf fan has seen Tiger's legendary **chip-in** on the 16th hole at Augusta in 2005, where the ball seemed to hang over the lip of the hole for an eternity before dropping in (if you haven't, then you need to look it up!), or Tiger's incredible win at the 2019 Masters when everyone had already counted him down and out.

Whether you believe that he is the greatest golfer of all time or not, no one can deny that he is the biggest superstar that golf has ever seen and has singlehandedly brought millions of new fans to the beautiful game of golf.

Eldrick Tont 'Tiger' Woods (of course Tiger isn't his real name!) was born in 1975, in Cypress, California to Earl and Kultida Woods. His father was one of the first African-American college baseball players in all of America, a single-digit **handicap** golfer *and* a US Army Officer who served two combat tours in the Vietnam War. He met Tiger's mother in her native Thailand during a tour of duty in 1968 (Tont is a traditional Thai name).

Earl was very ambitious for his son to be a sports star and boy did he luck out - young Tiger putted his first ball at just 10 months old when he could barely walk and was already playing golf regularly by the age of 2. He made his first TV appearance at 3 years old when he putted against the comedian Bob Hope and that same year, shot an astonishing 48 over nine holes (that's better than a lot of club players, and he was only three!).

A few more TV appearances and small tournament wins later, Tiger won his first big junior tournament when he won the 9-10 boys event at the Junior Golf World Championships at the age of eight. The world was getting its first glimpse of the future superstar.

Woods continued to go from strength to strength over the next few years, beating his father for the first time at the age of 11 and breaking 70 for the first time at 12. It was clear that Tiger was destined for greatness, but there was one thing that could get in the way of that - money. Tiger did not come from a wealthy family and golf can be a very expensive sport, so Tiger's parents made the incredibly brave decision to **re-mortgage** their house when Tiger was 14 in order to fund his golf career.

Thankfully it didn't take long for them to realise that this was a worthwhile investment because in 1991, just one year after, Tiger became the youngest winner ever of the US Junior Amateur Championship at 15 years old and was named the Golf Digest Junior Amateur Player of the Year!

No one had ever won the US Junior Amateur Championship twice, but Tiger showed the world that he was a talent never before seen and won it for three consecutive years! In 1994, Woods came from six shots behind to win the US Amateur Championships, which he also won for the following two years.

Tiger was already a hot commodity in the sports world by this point and many prestigious colleges were desperate for him to join them. He chose Stanford, who were the reigning NCAA champions and studied economics. It was during his time at Stanford that he played in his first PGA Tour major - the 1995 Masters. He finished in 41st, which was impressive for a debut, especially as he was the only amateur to **make the cut**. Tiger spent two years at college before turning professional in August 1996.

If you thought that he needed some time to adjust to life on the professional circuit, then think again. Tiger impressed immediately by winning two of the eight PGA events that he played as a pro that year. What was perhaps the most impressive thing about this young man's game was his ability to generate huge club-head speed, which meant that Tiger was regularly driving the ball over 300 yards. That may seem normal now, but in 1996 this was rare.

The year is now 1997 and the golfing world is about to change forever. Tiger was 21 coming into the Masters in red hot form. He stormed to victory, shooting a tournament record 270 (-18) and finished 12 strokes ahead of second place! This made him the youngest Masters winner in history, which is a record that he still holds. Tiger also became the first person of colour to win at the Masters, which showed every young child in the world that it doesn't matter what you look like or where you come from: you can still become the greatest golfer on the planet. Just two months later, he was ranked number one in the world for the first time, which is something he would get very used to in the future...

1998 was a bit of a tame year for Tiger's standards (he was still number one in the world for large parts of it), but this changed dramatically in 1999. He became the first golfer in 25 years to win eight PGA Tour events in one year. During this impressive run, he also picked up his second major at the PGA Championships where he finished one stroke ahead of the up-and-coming 19-year-old Sergio Garcia.

The year is now 2000, which may have been the year of the dragon in the Chinese zodiac, but for any golf fan old enough to remember, it was undoubtedly the year of the tiger. Woods started the year off by finishing fifth in The Masters before casually winning the US Open by 15 strokes (yes you read that right), tying Jack Nicklaus for the lowest US Open 72-hole score (272) in history and setting the record for the biggest winning margin at a major.

Tiger was now one major away from completing the **career Grand Slam**, which he could achieve by winning The Open a month later. Any other player may have felt the pressure at this point, but not Tiger. He breezed to victory, finishing 19 under **par** and eight strokes ahead of the rest of the field which meant that he was the youngest person ever to win all four majors.

The utter dominance by Tiger continued and he won the PGA Championships a few months later as well as The Masters in 2001. This meant that Tiger had now won all four majors in a row and is the only player in history who has achieved this. If they had all been won in the same calendar year, then this would have been known as a **calendar Grand Slam**, but they spanned over two years so this incredible run is now known as the "Tiger Slam".

Over the next eight years, Tiger continued to dominate the sport like never before. He set the record for the longest consecutive period being ranked number one in the world at 264 weeks from August 15th 1999 to September 4th 2004, before breaking his own record by being ranked world number one for 281 weeks from June 12th 2005 to October 30th 2010.

Despite requiring knee surgery in 2008, he won his 14th major at the US Open that same year to complete his third career Grand Slam (meaning he had won all four majors at least three times each). It seemed certain at this point that Tiger was going to break Jack Nicklaus' all-time major record of 18, but this is where Tiger's career took a major turn for the worse.

Tiger had a relatively innocent image of himself with the media up until this point, but a suspicious car crash outside of his home in Florida in November 2009 caused the media to start investigating greatly into his personal life. Tiger had been married to Swedish model Elin Nordegren since 2004, but they found out that he had been having regular extramarital affairs and this became global news.

Before this, Tiger had been loved by golf fans worldwide, but now it seemed that the whole world (and not just golf fans) was against him. This caused Tiger to take a break from golf to focus on his family, but things only got worse when he and Elin divorced the following year.

Tiger returned to golf after a six-month break, but it was clear that his game was not the same. He failed to win any tournaments in the next two years, before finally returning to winning ways at the Arnold Palmer Invitational in 2012.

The golfing world did see glimpses of the old Tiger over the next two years, and Tiger even won five PGA Tour events in 2013 which caused him to regain the world number one spot for another 60 weeks, but this was short-lived.

Just as Tiger looked to be regaining his form of old, he started to get severe back pain, and it was clear that he could not swing the club freely. From 2014 until 2018, Woods was forced to play just a handful of tournaments, missing the 2016 season entirely. He underwent multiple back surgeries, and the golfing world was no longer worried that he wouldn't win another major, but worried that he would not be able to play golf at all.

He returned to the PGA Tour in 2018 and to the relief of everyone, was able to play the full season on tour. Tiger even won his first PGA Tour event in five years at the Tour Championship. It was a miracle that Tiger was playing well enough to win again after everything he had gone through. But not even the most die-hard

Tiger Woods fans dared to believe what would happen in 2019.

In perhaps the greatest moment in sporting history, Tiger defied all the odds to win the 2019 Masters, finishing one shot ahead of the pack on 13 under par. It had been eleven years since Tiger won his last major championship and, at the age of 43, this made Tiger the second oldest winner of the Masters of all time (behind a certain Jack Nicklaus). Simply unbelievable!

Tiger capped off his remarkable 2019 by winning his 82nd PGA Tour event at the Zozo Championship, tying him for the all-time record with Sam Snead.

Sadly this run of good health and form didn't last long. Tiger was forced to undergo more back surgery in 2021 before being involved in another car crash that had the whole golfing world worried. His right leg had to be surgically rebuilt, and there were serious doubts about whether he would be able to walk freely again, let alone swing a golf club.

In true Tiger fashion, he defied the odds once again and returned to the PGA Tour in 2022 where he played at the Masters. Tiger was clearly not his old self and was in visible pain walking around the golf course but somehow he still made the cut. Since then we have seen brief glimpses of Tiger playing in the Majors, once again making the cut at the 2023 and 2024 Masters, but his physical condition still seems far from what it was before the accident.

Tiger's grit and determination over the last few years has been absolutely incredible and his passion for the game is a true inspiration to all those watching. We can only hope that his body returns to a level where he can compete at the very top once again.

Tiger has broken almost every record there is in golf over his career and has taken golf to a level that people never thought was possible. Not only has he been incredible on the course, but he has also been an inspiration off the course by being the first person of colour to succeed in the sport.

He has shown that it doesn't matter what you look like, or how much money you grow up with, because with hard work and dedication, anyone can make it to the very top of golf. His Masters win in 2019 is not only one of golf's most incredible moments in history, but also one of sport's greatest comebacks. He has proven time and time again that just when you think his victory days are over, he is capable of more, so who knows what the future will bring!

# GARY PLAYER

## MAJORS

**THE OPEN CHAMPIONSHIP**
X3

**PGA CHAMPIONSHIP**
X2

**US OPEN**
X1

**THE MASTERS**
X3

**TOTAL MAJORS**
9

## CAREER STATS

| | |
|---|---|
| PROFESSIONAL WINS | 159 |
| PGA TOUR WINS | 24 |
| EUROPEAN TOUR WINS | 4 |
| SUNSHINE TOUR WINS | 20 |
| PGA TOUR CHAMPIONS | 22 |
| EUROPEAN SENIOR TOUR | 3 |
| WORLD GOLF HALL OF FAME INDUCTION | 1974 |

| BIOGRAPHY | BORN | NOVEMBER 1, 1935 |
| --- | --- | --- |
| | NATIONALITY | SOUTH AFRICAN |
| | TURNED PRO | 1953 |
| | HEIGHT | 1.68 M (5 FT 6 IN) |
| | PLAYS | RIGHT-HANDED |

Gary Player is a true legend of the game whose name will live on forever in golf. He played in one of the most competitive eras in golf's history, regularly going up against legends such as Jack Nicklaus and Arnold Palmer (you will read about both of these later on), and still won an impressive nine majors. Not only this, but he became the third player in history to complete the Grand Slam and the first non-American to do so. It is no wonder that he was voted Sportsman of the Century in South Africa in 2000!

Unfortunately, Gary also had some very controversial and backwards opinions as a younger man which cannot be ignored. There is no space in the world today for views such as these, but luckily Gary came to his senses many years ago and now realises how wrong those opinions were.

Gary was born in Johannesburg, South Africa in November 1935 to Harry and Muriel Player. He didn't have it easy as a child: his mother died of cancer when he was only 8 years old and his father worked in the mines so was often away from home. The Players didn't have much money and his father even had to take out a loan to buy Gary's first set of golf clubs.

It wasn't until Gary was 14 that he started to play golf, which he did at The Virginia Park golf course in Johannesburg. This may seem quite late to start golf compared to some of the others on this list, but Gary's talent was so extraordinary that it didn't take him long to catch up. In fact, he even parred the first three holes in his first full round of golf. It was clear from the start that Gary Player was born to be a golfer. He continued to progress at an alarmingly fast rate and just three years after he started, he turned pro in 1953 at the age of 17.

Gary's first five years on the tour were relatively slow as he was still learning and developing his game. He finally got his first PGA Tour victory in 1958 at the Kentucky Derby Open and the world finally started to notice the young South African.

Despite not winning any big-time tournaments on the golf course for the first five years of his pro career, he did have the biggest win that one can have off the course in 1957 when he married childhood sweetheart, Vivienne Verwey. The pair had six children together, and Vivienne, the six children, a tutor, and a nanny would often all come to Gary's tournaments when he was older - so Gary was never short of supporters! But, anyway, back to the young Gary's golf career.

The year is now 1959 and 23-year-old Gary Player is about to announce himself to the golfing world on the biggest stage. He produced a miraculous performance to win the Open Championship, coming from four shots back on the final day to win the tournament by two strokes and take home the winner's check of £1,000. Despite a nervy **double bogey** on the 18th, Gary had finally done it. He had won his first major in stunning style.

Many golfers take their foot off the gas after their first major win and struggle to live up to the expectation, but not Gary.

He came into the 1961 Masters on good form and was considered a serious contender but by no means the favourite. Arnold Palmer had won the tournament for two of the previous three years and, up until this point, no foreigner had won the Masters, so the odds were certainly stacked against our talented South African.

Player and Palmer battled it out over the first three days, but Gary had a four-shot lead after 54 holes and looked set to win his second major. However, the final round would prove to be anything but a routine win. Gary shot an unconvincing final round of 74 to finish on eight under and came into the clubhouse nearly an hour ahead of Palmer. As Palmer had done so many times in his career, he turned on the screws when it mattered most and came into the par four 18th one stroke ahead of Player, needing just a par to win the tournament. To everyone's amazement, Palmer cracked under the pressure and double-bogeyed the last. This made Player the first non-American Masters winner in history!

This incredible victory, along with two other PGA titles that year, helped Gary to be the leading money winner of the PGA Tour in 1961 and showed that he really was one of the best.

Things would only get harder the following year and that is because a certain Jack Nicklaus was announcing himself to the world and Palmer was still dominating. Nicklaus had beaten Player in an 18-hole **playoff** at the

1962 US Open to win his first major, and Palmer had won the other two majors so it seemed that Gary had to accept that he was the third-best golfer of the year.

As always, Gary proved the critics wrong. He won the final major of the year at the 1962 PGA Championship by one stroke, finishing the tournament on two under par. Player had now won three majors and was only one win away from the Career Grand Slam.

Gary had to wait three more years for his dream to come true, but it finally happened when he won the 1965 US Open. Although it looked like plain sailing for much of the tournament for Player, he made his fans sweat at the end. He had a three-shot lead with three to play, but amazingly needed an 18-hole playoff to lift the title over Kel Nagle.

This win made him the first non-American to win the tournament in 38 years, and more importantly, made him the third player at the time to have completed the Career Grand Slam, which he did at just 29 years old! This would have been impressive in any era of golf, but to have achieved this whilst competing against such formidable rivals (Arnold Palmer and Jack Nicklaus) was simply phenomenal.

Unfortunately, it was also at this time that Player showed his support for **Apartheid** in South Africa. This was a regime that treated black South Africans in an unforgivable way from 1948 to 1994, so to see Player voice his support for it was truly devastating. This narrow-minded thinking rightly tarnished his reputation and people started protesting at his tournaments, but he did not receive the backlash at the time that these opinions deserved. The world was different back then and racism was not only present in everyday life, but generally accepted. This is the world that a young Tiger Woods entered, fiercely and bravely, and it's important to remember just how far we've come as a society.

Over the next 13 years, Player won five more major titles and became the only player to have won the Open Championship in three separate decades.

Perhaps the most memorable of these victories was his last at the 1978 Masters. Player came into the final round seven strokes behind the leader in a tie for tenth. He shot one of the all-time greatest rounds in Masters history, with **birdies** on seven of the last ten holes, shooting a back nine 30 and an overall 64 to win the **Green Jacket** one shot ahead of the pack on 11-under. This made him the oldest player at the time to have won the Masters, doing so at 42 years old.

Rather than slow down and retire as he grew older, Gary took his talents to the Champions Tour in 1985 and unsurprisingly became one of the most successful players on this tour in history. He has won over 30 times worldwide including nine Senior Majors. This means that he has won 18 Majors on the PGA Tour and the Champions Tour combined!

He competed for his 52nd and final time at the Masters in 2009 which is another of his many records, and only missed one year since 1957 which was due to injury. There is a reason that people call him Mr. Fitness!

Gary finally saw sense in the 1980s and completely changed his views on Apartheid in South Africa. He recognised what a terrible and unfair system it was and spoke about how the South African government had 'brainwashed' people such as himself into supporting it.

In his retirement, he created the Player Foundation which provided education, food, medicine and sports for poor children living in South Africa. It has donated $65 million to improve the lives of the same children that the Apartheid regime had intended to deprive, so I think it's clear to say that he feels more than a little bit guilty for his prior opinions.

While it's not up to me to decide whether he is forgiven, let this be a lesson that **prejudiced** opinions will stain you for the rest of your life. They will follow you long after you've learnt the error of your ways, so be careful with the things you say. Don't let a moment of **ignorance** lessen your achievements!

Gary is undoubtedly one of the greatest players of all time and his battles with Jack Nicklaus and Arnold Palmer will live on forever in golf. It is a great shame that his legacy has been tarnished by the views he had at the start of his golf career, but over the last 40 years, he has done everything possible to try and right these wrongs. There is no question that the Player Foundation has changed the lives of thousands of people and none of that would have been possible without Gary.

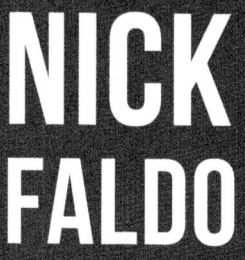

# NICK
## FALDO

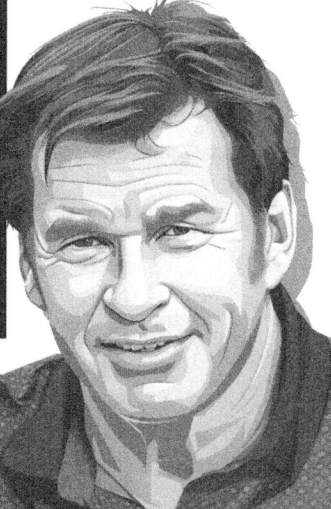

## MAJORS

THE OPEN
CHAMPIONSHIP
X3

PGA
CHAMPIONSHIP
X0

US OPEN
X0

THE MASTERS
X3

TOTAL MAJORS
6

## CAREER STATS

| | |
|---|---|
| PROFESSIONAL WINS | 43 |
| PGA TOUR WINS | 9 |
| EUROPEAN TOUR WINS | 30 |
| RYDER CUP RECORD | 23-19-4 |
| PGA PLAYER OF THE YEAR | 1 |
| SUNSHINE TOUR WINS | 1 |

| PGA WIN % | PRIZE MONEY |
|---|---|
| 9/306 (2.9%) | $6,045,627 |

Ryder Cup record is in the format of wins-losses-halves

| BORN | JULY 18, 1957 |
|---|---|
| NATIONALITY | ENGLISH |
| TURNED PRO | 1976 |
| HEIGHT | 1.91 M (6 FT 3 IN) |
| PLAYS | RIGHT-HANDED |

Nick Faldo was one of the leading names in the golfing world in the late 1980s and early 1990s, and it wasn't just in the majors where he excelled (although he did win six of these as well). He is a Ryder Cup legend who sits second in the all-time points list with 25, ranks fifth all-time for European Tour wins with 30 *and* was ranked number one in the world for 97 weeks!

Alongside Seve Ballesteros (who will be coming up later), Nick is surely one of the greatest European players of recent times.

Born in Welwyn Garden City, Hertfordshire, England, in July 1957, Nick was the only child of Joyce and George Faldo. He too was introduced to golf later than most, in fact, he didn't have an interest in the sport at all until he watched the great Jack Nicklaus win the 1971 Masters at the age of 13. The thrill of competition and **sportsmanship** was enough to spark interest in this legend in the making.

As with Gary Player, Nick played his first round of golf at 14, and just a few years later he had convinced his parents to let him quit school to pursue his golf career (don't get any ideas kids!). His hard work soon paid off and two years later, in 1974, he was selected to play in the English Amateur. While he didn't win it this year, he came back one year later to win both the tournament and the British Youths Open Amateur

Championship!

Faldo was making a name for himself worldwide and was offered a scholarship to the University of Houston. Although this seemed a great opportunity for Nick, he felt that the schoolwork would get in the way of his golf so he quit after just ten weeks. It was clear that he was ready to make the jump to the big leagues so in 1976, he turned pro and joined the European Professional Golfers Association.

Faldo performed consistently well throughout the first few years of his pro career. He won his first European Tour event at the Skol Lager Individual in 1977 and followed this up with another win at the Colgate PGA Championship the following year. On top of this, he was selected for the 1977 Ryder Cup team at just 20 years old, becoming the youngest Ryder Cup player in history at the time. He even won all three of his matches including a historic win over Jack Nicklaus, the very man who inspired him to play golf!

Faldo didn't stop there: he played in every Ryder Cup over the following years and only went one year without winning a European Tour event. He also finished top of the European Tour Order of Merit in 1983 after winning a superb five European Tour titles.

Despite these impressive results, Faldo was struggling to make an impact on the biggest stage that golf has to offer - the majors. His best finish from 1976-1984 at a major was a tie for fourth place at The Open in 1982, and this included a catastrophic collapse at the 1984 Masters where he led at one point in the final round, only to finish in a meagre 15th. This earned Nick the unfortunate nickname of 'Nicky Fold'o' from the British media who believed that he did not have what it took to win a major.

Many golfers would have been happy with a career like this (after all, he did just win five tournaments in one year) but Nick knew that he could do better than this. He knew that he should not only be competing for majors but winning them. And lots of them at that.

Something had to change, so Faldo made the very brave decision to alter his swing in a gamble that could have gone either way. Nick had always had a beautiful-looking long swing, but he believed that it was unreliable in high-pressure moments and he used too much wrist. He decided to work with legendary golf coach David Leadbetter and together they made his swing more tight and compact.

Naturally, it took a few years for Nick to adjust to this new swing, but boy did it pay off when he did.

Nick's new and improved swing helped him to hold his nerve incredibly at the 1987 Open Championship, where he shot 18 consecutive pars in the final round to finish one ahead of the pack on five under par. He had finally done it! He had proved everyone wrong and shown that he could perform under the most intense pressure.

This win kickstarted an incredible run of form and confidence for Nick. Over seven years from 1987-1993, Nick won the Open three times, finished runner-up once, and also finished third once. His success with his new swing didn't just apply to the Open, he also won the Masters three times in 1989, 1990, and 1996 and finished in second at both the US Open and the PGA Championship. This final win at the Masters is a particularly memorable tournament: Nick trailed tournament leader Greg Norman by six shots coming into the final round, but an impressive final round 67 from Faldo and a catastrophic 78 blow-up from Norman meant that Nick eased to the win by five strokes!

Faldo continued to play many golf events well in the 2000s and played in his final Open in 2015 before deciding it was time to hang up his clubs.

It was not just on the golf course where Faldo had an impact on the golfing world. He has designed many golf courses, coached at schools and pro shops, launched the Faldo Series which gives opportunities to young golfers and has been a regular commentator for the BBC. Faldo was also selected as captain of the European Ryder Cup team in 2008, although this role proved not to be very successful and his Europe team lost 16½ – 11½ to the USA.

Nick's incredible golf career should be seen as a true inspiration to us all. He went *years* without major success and was told by many that he never would, yet he didn't listen. He persevered, put the work in and succeeded, and that's a lesson that you can apply to any area of life.

# LOUISE SUGGS

## MAJORS

WESTERN OPEN
**X4**

TITLEHOLDERS
CHAMPIONSHIP
**X4**

CHEVRON
CHAMPIONSHIP
**X0**

WOMEN'S PGA
CHAMPIONSHIP
**X1**

US WOMEN'S OPEN
**X2**

**TOTAL MAJORS
11**

## CAREER STATS

| | |
|---|---|
| PROFESSIONAL WINS | 61 |
| LPGA TOUR WINS | 61 |
| WORLD GOLF HALL OF FAME INDUCTION | 1951 |
| LPGA VARE TROPHY | 1 |
| LPGA TOUR MONEY WINNER | 2 |
| PATTY BERG AWARD | 1 |
| BOB JONES AWARD | 1 |

# BIOGRAPHY

| | |
|---|---|
| BORN | SEPTEMBER 7, 1923 |
| NATIONALITY | AMERICAN |
| TURNED PRO | 1948 |
| HEIGHT | 1.68 M (5 FT 6 IN) |
| PLAYS | RIGHT-HANDED |

Louise Suggs is not only one of the greatest golfers of all time, but she is a true pioneer of women's golf. Her golf statistics alone are comfortably enough to include her in this book: she won a staggering 11 majors, 61 times on the LPGA Tour as well as winning many prestigious amateur events. However, her contributions to the LPGA Tour and growing women's golf worldwide mean that her name will be immortalised in golf history forever.

Mae Louise Suggs was born in Atlanta, Georgia, on the 7th of September 1923 into a very sporty family. Her father was a former professional baseball player who then turned to building golf courses, and her grandfather owned the Atlanta Crackers, a very successful baseball team. Sport clearly ran through her veins and she was destined for sporting greatness right from the start.

Suggs first started to play golf at the age of 10 on a course both designed and managed by her father, and her talent was clear right away. She progressed very quickly, and just six years later, she won the prestigious Georgia State Amateur. If anyone thought this early success was a fluke, they were soon proven wrong and the young Louise Suggs went on to have one of the most successful amateur golf careers there has ever been.

She won so many prestigious amateur events that there would be too many to list here, but some of the biggest wins included the Southern Amateur Championship in both 1941 and 1947, the Women's Western Open in both 1946 and 1947 and the Titleholders Championship in 1946.

These final two tournaments may sound familiar to you, and that's because they are now considered majors by the LPGA. However, the LPGA didn't exist until 1950, so they were still considered as amateur events at this time. This means that Suggs had technically already won three majors during her amateur career, but she wouldn't be awarded with these until a few years later.

Despite being one of the best golfers in the world, Suggs was barely making any money from the sport. You have to remember that times were very different in this era and women were not treated with the respect or recognition that they deserved, especially in sports. She even regularly put her own **purse** up at tournaments and would joke that it would make her try even harder to win because she wanted to win her own money back.

Suggs made her first appearance for the United States at the Curtis Cup in a 6 ½ 2 ½ victory in 1948 and turned pro shortly after. She immediately accepted a sponsorship contract to endorse MacGregor golf, which meant she could finally earn some proper money from golf which she so desperately deserved.

Her next ten years as a professional golfer would be some of the most dominating that golf has ever seen.

She won another eight majors (bringing her total up to eleven) and built fierce rivalries with fellow legends Babe Zaharias and Patty Berg (who you will read about later in this book). Perhaps Suggs' most impressive win of her career was at the 1949 US Women's Open where she beat second-placed Zaharias by a whopping 14 strokes! Another historic moment for Suggs came at the 1957 LPGA Championship, where a three-stroke victory made her the first LPGA player in history to win a career Grand Slam - what an achievement!

On top of these victories at majors, she also won the Vare trophy in 1957, as well as finishing as the leading money winner on the LPGA Tour in 1953 and 1960.

Now, here's what makes Louise's career even more impressive. While she was busy breaking records on the course, she was also very busy developing and growing the LPGA.

As we mentioned earlier, the LPGA was founded in 1950, but we did not mention that Louise was one of the original 13 founders. On top of this, she served as the President of the LPGA from 1955-1957 and was the first to be inducted into the LPGA Tour Hall of Fame in 1951 alongside Patty Berg, Betty Jameson, and Babe Zaharias.

Suggs constantly strived to grow golf for women and she believed that, if they were given a fair chance to go from tee to green in the same number of strokes, they could both compete and win against men. She was given her chance to prove this in 1961 at a mixed game in Palm Beach, Florida, where she beat many professional male players, including all-time golf great

Sam Snead.

Suggs retired from professional golf in 1962 but remained very active in the game. She regularly taught golf in clinics after retirement and competed on the senior LPGA Tour for many decades to come.

Suggs received countless honours and awards after her retirement, including receiving the highest award given by the United States Golf Association, the Bob Jones Award, in 2007. Perhaps the most special was the award named after her - the Louise Suggs Trophy - which was created by the LPGA in 2000 and is given to the Rookie of the Year. Imagine having your own award named after you, that's when you know you are a true legend of golf!

Louise's career is incredible for so many different reasons. Her eleven major victories and 61 LPGA Tour wins put her right up there with the best of all time, and this, combined with her contributions to the LPGA Tour, means that her name will live on in golfing legend forever.

# SAM SNEAD

## MAJORS

**THE OPEN CHAMPIONSHIP**
X1

**PGA CHAMPIONSHIP**
X3

**US OPEN**
X0

**THE MASTERS**
X3

**TOTAL MAJORS**
7

## CAREER STATS

| | |
|---|---|
| PROFESSIONAL WINS | 142 |
| PGA TOUR WINS | 82 |
| RYDER CUP RECORD | (10–2–1) |
| WORLD GOLF HALL OF FAME INDUCTION | 1974 |
| PGA GOLFER OF THE YEAR | 1 |

| PGA WIN % | PRIZE MONEY |
|---|---|
| 82/585 (14%) | $713,155 |

Ryder Cup record is in the format of wins-losses-halves

| BORN | MAY 27, 1912 |
| --- | --- |
| NATIONALITY | AMERICAN |
| TURNED PRO | 1934 |
| HEIGHT | 1.80 M (5 FT 11 IN) |
| PLAYS | RIGHT-HANDED |

Slammin' Sam Snead may have been born well over 100 years ago, but his name is still known by golf fans all around the world, and for good reason. Snead is the joint all-time record holder for most PGA Tour wins with Tiger on 82 (although Tiger will be looking to change that), holds the record for the most wins at a single event with eight at the Greater Greensboro Open, and is also recognised as being the first person in history to break 60 in tournament play with a round of 59 at the Greenbrier Open in 1959!

Snead is also famous for always rocking his iconic straw hat and, unbelievably, never having a golf lesson. How crazy is that!

Sam Snead was born in May 1912, in Ashwood Virginia into a poor farming family. Sam's older brother Homer was very into sports, in particular golf, which had a big impact on the young Snead. Just like many young golfers in this day, he started caddying and helping out at his local 9-hole course in order to make a bit of money.

Whenever Sam wasn't helping out, he could be found practising for hours each day with battered homemade clubs, starting to perfect that flawless swing that he would soon become famous for. Back in the 1920s golf was seen as an elitist sport that was supposed to only be played by the 'rich' (which is clearly nonsense).

Sam, who came from a poor family, wore tatty clothes and could not afford to buy clubs, took special pride in having the best swing at the golf course and posting rounds that many of the members could only dream of.

Sam's game continued to progress incredibly fast as a young man, and by the time he was 22, he was good enough to turn pro. I'm sure that many of those old club members were eating their words at this point.

Sam's first few years as a pro were incredibly successful and it was clear that he was a very special player in the making. His first tournament win came in 1936 when he won the West Virginia Closed Pro and he followed this up a month later with the first of his 17 wins (yes, you read that right, 17 wins!) at the West Virginia Open. These impressive results earned him the right to play on the PGA Tour in 1937.

Just as we would expect from the man who would soon become the all-time record winner on the PGA Tour, it did not take him long at all to start dominating. Snead won five PGA Tour events in his first year, and by the time he had spent five years on the PGA Tour, he had already racked up 26 wins! He also won the first of his four Vardon Trophies in 1939 for the best scoring average on the PGA Tour, showing that he truly was one of the best in the world.

Despite his complete dominance on the Tour, there was still a big hole in Snead's trophy cabinet, and that was of course a major win. In fact, Sam had come second in four majors from 1937-1940 and it seemed that he may not have the nerves to win at the highest level of golf.

By 1942 World War II was well underway and the majority of golf tournaments were no longer taking place. Little did Snead know that when he entered the 1942 PGA Championship, this would be the last major before the end of the war in 1945 and therefore his last shot at a title for years. Despite all the added pressure, Snead did not let this opportunity slip. He beat Jim Turnesa 2 & 1 in the final match (the PGA Championship was **match play** until 1958) to win the first of his seven majors.

The boy who grew up in a poor farming family and had to make his own golf clubs was now a major champion. Incredible!

Snead served in the US Navy over the next three years, and in total was forced to miss 14 majors due to the war. However, if anyone thought that Snead would have lost his edge over this period, they were sorely mistaken.

From 1946-1954 Snead went on to win six majors, which included three wins at the Masters, one at the Open and two more at the PGA Championships. During this period, Snead had one of the most incredible years that has ever been seen on the Tour. In 1950 he won 11 tournaments, as well as having an average of 69.23 over 96 rounds, which are numbers that have rarely been seen since.

Snead continued to have success in golf for many years to come and many have praised his longevity in the sport. His final win on the PGA Tour came in 1965 when he won the Greater Greensboro Open for a record eighth time at the age of 52. This made him the oldest winner on the PGA Tour and he still shares the record with Tiger for most wins at a single PGA Tour event.

Snead continued to defy his age much later in his life. At 62, he came third at the 1974 PGA Championship, just three strokes behind winner Lee Trevino. At 71, he shot a 12-under-par 60 at The Homestead in Hot Springs, Virginia, and at the age of 85, it is said that he was still able to break 80. It is many golfer's dream to shoot a better score than their age. Well, for Sam Snead, he was able to beat his age by 11 strokes!

The only major that Sam never managed to win was the US Open, but this wasn't for a lack of chances. He was one stroke ahead of the field going into the final hole of the last round at the 1939 US Open, but he was not aware of this and thought that he needed a birdie to win. He played the hole too aggressively, and inexplicably **triple-bogeyed** the last to finish in fifth place. Later in his career in 1947, he missed another golden opportunity to complete the career slam when he was leading by two strokes with three to play over Lew Worsham, but it was just not to be.

Despite never quite getting over the line at the US Open, there is no denying that Snead is one of the greatest golfers of all time. His seven major victories put him right up there with the best, but his 82 PGA Tour victories, 142 professional wins and four Vardon trophies show that very few in history have achieved a level of dominance that Sam Snead did throughout his long career.

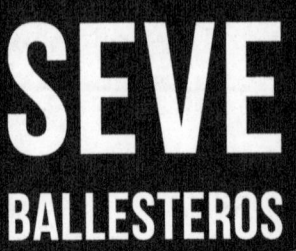

# SEVE
## BALLESTEROS

## MAJORS

**THE OPEN CHAMPIONSHIP**
X3

**PGA CHAMPIONSHIP**
X0

**US OPEN**
X0

**THE MASTERS**
X2

**TOTAL MAJORS**
5

## CAREER STATS

| | |
|---|---|
| WEEKS AT NO. 1 | 61 |
| PROFESSIONAL WINS | 90 |
| PGA TOUR WINS | 9 |
| EUROPEAN TOUR WINS | 50 |
| RYDER CUP RECORD | 20-12-5 |
| EUROPEAN TOUR GOLFER OF THE YEAR | 3 |
| WORLD GOLF HALL OF FAME INDUCTION | 1999 |

# BIOGRAPHY

| | |
|---|---|
| BORN | 9 APRIL 1957 |
| NATIONALITY | SPANISH |
| TURNED PRO | 1974 |
| HEIGHT | 1.83 M (6 FT 0 IN) |
| PLAYS | RIGHT-HANDED |

Seve Ballesteros' flamboyant and dazzling style of play was loved by millions of fans worldwide and it is a tragedy that he was taken from us at such a young age. The beloved Spaniard may have won the joint least amount of majors on this list (5), but he contributed to golf in so many other ways and most definitely deserves his place on this list as one of the greatest golfers of all time.

Seve's achievements in golf cannot be understated: he's comfortably in first place for the most European Tour wins (50), spent 61 weeks ranked at world number one and is an all-time European Ryder Cup legend!

Severiano Ballesteros Sota was born in a small fishing village called Pedreña in northern Spain in April 1957. He was born into a relatively poor family and was the youngest of five brothers, so money was tight for the boys growing up.

Golf ran in the blood of the Ballesteros family. His uncle Ramón Sota had been the Spanish champion four times and even finished sixth at the Masters in 1965, so it's no surprise that all three of Seve's brothers became golf professionals. They all achieved impressive results on their own, but none came close to the legendary status that Seve achieved.

Despite golf being so important to the family, they didn't have the money to buy Seve a membership to the golf course that their house conveniently looked over, or even any of his own golf clubs. Many kids would have given up on their dreams of playing golf at this point, but not Seve. He was simply born to play golf and would do anything to make this happen.

At the age of eight, he found a discarded club head and attached it to a stick to make his own makeshift club, which he used to practice on a local beach or on the golf course at night. Eventually, his older brother Manuel gave him an old 3-iron, so he finally had his own proper club to practice with.

By the time he was ten, he was old enough to start working as a **caddie** which gave him the chance to play in the caddie championships. Despite a dreadful ten on the first hole, Seve came back to shoot 51 over 9 holes and win the tournament which officially allowed him to use the course for free!

It's no surprise that his game now began to progress quickly: at the age of 12, he won the same event again with an 18-hole score of 79 and just one year later he shot a 65. Seve continued to go from strength to strength as a junior, and just short of his 17th birthday in 1974, he turned pro.

The young Spaniard still had a lot to learn before he could start competing with the best. His first two years started slow, with Seve even recording an 89 in the first round at the Portuguese Open, but his results started picking up nicely. At the end of 1975, he was ranked as Spain's number-one player under 25.

People were starting to recognise the name of the exciting young Spanish golfer by this point, but 1976 would be the year when every golf fan would see the future star that he was going to be.

Seve was playing in just his second major at the 1976 Open, but came as close as you can get to winning. He held a two-shot lead going into the final round, but a 66 from Johnny Miller meant that Seve had to settle for a tie for second with Jack Nicklaus. Seve's opposition had been too good on the day, but it was clear that he would win many majors in the future.

Just one month after this close call, Seve won his first European Tour event at the Dutch Open by eight strokes, which helped him to win the first of his six European Tour Order of Merit titles (awarded to the leading money winner on the European Tour for that year).

After this breakthrough year, Seve never let up on the European Tour again. He astonishingly won at least one European Tour event each year from 1976-1992, with 1986 being his standout year where he won a record *six* tournaments. There has never been any other player who has dominated the European Tour like Seve did over these years, and there probably never will be!

Despite all his success on the European Tour, Seve knew that in order to be considered as one of the greatest golfers of all time, he had to perform at the majors as well. It had been three years since he squandered a two-stroke lead going into the final round of the Open, and the sting of defeat could still be felt. The stakes were high but Seve delivered, coming back from two strokes behind on the final to finish three strokes ahead of both Jack Nicklaus and Ben Crenshaw. He had won the 1979 Open Championship! What made this final round even more incredible was that he hit his tee shot into the car park on the 16th hole, only to make one of the greatest **up-and-downs** in golf history to make a birdie (go and watch it on YouTube!).

Not only had he proven that he was the best player on the European Tour, but also that he was one of the best in the world who could beat some of the greatest players in history.

He went on to win The Open two more times in 1984 and 1988, as well as winning the Masters in 1980 and 1983. His 1980 win at the Masters was iconic for two reasons: he was the first European player to ever win the competition, and at just 23 years old, he was the youngest Masters winner in history.

Seve was not done making history there - he was a member of the first-ever Ryder Cup squad in 1979 where the team included European golfers (rather than just British ones). The United States had won the last 10 Ryder Cups at this point, but this dominance would soon change when the likes of Seve Ballesteros came onto the team. He played in eight Ryder Cups from 1979-1995, winning it four times and winning an incredible 22.5 out of a possible 37 points.

He was also part of the most successful Ryder Cup partnership in history, alongside fellow Spanish golfing legend José María Olazábal. The pair played 15 matches against the Americans, winning eleven, tying two and only losing two matches.

But wait... Seve's Ryder Cup career isn't done there. He came back as European captain in 1997, leading them to an incredibly tense 14 ½ 13 ½ win at the Valderrama Golf Club in his home country Spain, in the first European Ryder Cup held outside of the British Isles. The man is a walking record book!

Seve continued to play golf until 2007, but soon began to struggle with back injuries. He won his 50th and final European Tour event in 1995 and was inducted into the Golf World Hall of Fame in 1999.

In his personal life, Seve was married to Carmen Botín O'Shea from 1988 until their divorce in 2004 and the pair had three children together.

In one of the most devastating events to rock the golf world, Seve was diagnosed with brain cancer just one year after his retirement in 2008. He fought this illness for three years before tragically passing away on the 7th of May, 2011, at the age of 54.

The boy who grew up playing golf on beaches with a homemade club grew up to be one of the most liked and respected golfers in history. Seve should act as an inspiration to us all that if we are dedicated and work hard enough to achieve our goals, then anything is possible. His early death was an absolute tragedy, but Seve's name will live on forever in the record books and highlight-reels of golf.

# ANNIKA SÖRENSTAM

## MAJORS

DU MAURIER CLASSIC
**X0**

WOMEN'S BRITISH OPEN
**X1**

CHEVRON CHAMPIONSHIP
**X3**

WOMEN'S PGA CHAMPIONSHIP
**X3**

US WOMEN'S OPEN
**X3**

| TOTAL MAJORS |
|:---:|
| 10 |

## CAREER STATS

| | |
|---|---:|
| WEEKS AT NO. 1 | 60 |
| PROFESSIONAL WINS | 97 |
| LPGA TOUR WINS | 72 |
| LADIES EUROPEAN TOUR | 17 |
| SOLHEIM CUP RECORD | 22-11-4 |
| LPGA TOUR PLAYER OF THE YEAR | 8 |

| LPGA WIN % | PRIZE MONEY |
|:---:|:---:|
| 72/307 (23%) | $22,583,693 |

Solheim Cup record is in the format of wins-losses-halves

| BORN | OCTOBER 9, 1970 |
| NATIONALITY | SWEDISH |
| TURNED PRO | 1992 |
| HEIGHT | 1.68 M (5 FT 6 IN) |
| PLAYS | RIGHT-HANDED |

Where can we even begin with Annika Sörenstam? Considered by many to be the greatest LPGA player of all time, we would be here for hours if we tried to list all the records that she accumulated over her career.

Annika won a staggering 72 LPGA Tour events from 1995-2008, including 10 majors, putting her at third and fourth in the all-time leaderboards respectively. Not only was she a serial winner, but she performed so consistently well that it was scary. Annika won the Vare Trophy six times and still holds the record for the lowest season-long scoring average of 68.69, won the LPGA Player of the Year eight times and still holds the all-time LPGA money list record with $22,583,693 in winnings. But wait... I've saved the coolest for last. She is the only woman in history to shoot an official sub-60 round of golf when she shot a 59 at the Moon Valley Country Club, and she still has the nickname Ms. 59 to this day. Incredible!

Annika was born to Tom and Gunilla Sörenstam in a town near Stockholm, Sweden in October 1970. Her younger sister, Charlotta, would also one day become an incredibly successful golfer, with three professional wins to her name (including one on the LPGA Tour). The pair became the first two sisters to earn over $1 million dollars from golf. What a talented family!

It's no surprise that Annika was a sporty child, however

her focus was tennis, football and skiing (that's right, golf wasn't even one of her top 3 sports!). It's hard to believe for us mere mortals, but for young Annika, excelling in a whole variety of sports felt natural. She even got to number 12 in the country in tennis as a junior, and was so good at skiing that her coach urged her family to move to Northern Sweden to pursue a skiing career. Luckily for the golfing world, she started playing golf at the age of 12, and from then on, there was no other sport for her.

Annika and Charlotta started playing at a local 9-hole course and shared a set of clubs. Annika got the odd numbers and her sister got the even numbers, and with this makeshift set, she got her first handicap of 54.

As with so many on this list, Annika was an immediate star. However, there was one thing that held the young Annika back: confidence. She used to be so nervous about giving a victory speech at tournaments that she would deliberately three-putt the last few holes to come second and avoid public speaking. Eventually, her coaches realised what she was doing and they changed the rules so that both first and second place had to give a speech. This worked, and Annika realised that if she would have to speak anyway, then she might as well win.

With many of her confidence issues behind her, she started winning some big tournaments and people were beginning to notice her. She became a member of the Swedish National Golf Team from 1987-1992 which helped her to be scouted by the University of Arizona in 1991.

In years gone past, she might have been scared to move to a new country, but this was a new and determined Annika and she was ready to take the challenge head on. She won seven college titles in her first year and topped it off by becoming the first non-American and the first freshman to win the individual NCAA Division I Championship.

Annika was simply too good to stay at college, so the following year (1992), she turned professional.

Her life as a pro golfer had a stuttering start when she missed her LPGA **Tour card** by one stroke, forcing her to start on the Ladies European Tour. She didn't let this get her down, and became the Ladies European Tour Rookie of the Year in her first year, before being given her LPGA Tour card in 1994.

Annika had been given the chance that she needed and she was about to show the world that she belonged right at the top. She finished in second place at the Women's British Open, as well as earning two other top 10 finishes, which once again earned her the Rookie of the Year award, but this time on the LPGA.

It did not take her long to go one better at a major. Just one year later, and appearing at just her second US Women's Open, she pipped Meg Mallon by one stroke to become the champion.

The next five years of her career were still incredibly impressive, but by Annika's standards, we knew she was capable of more. She defended her title at the US Women's Open, won the LPGA Player of the Year award in 1997 and 1998 and became the first woman in history to finish a season with a scoring average of below 70 which she did in 1998 with an average of 69.99.

2001-2006 saw a period of golfing dominance that the LPGA Tour had not seen in 50 years. She won eight more majors, completing the career Grand Slam in 2003 when she won the Women's British Open, finished as LPGA Player of the Year for five consecutive years and won three Vare trophies, including that record-breaking one that we spoke about earlier.

Annika broke even more ground in 2003 when she became the first golfer since Babe Zaharias (we will get to her later) to compete in the PGA Tour. She put up a valiant performance, finishing in 96th out of 111 and lead the field in driving accuracy after the first round. Unfortunately, her putting let her down on the day but she well and truly showed that she could not just compete with, but beat the men.

Annika also had a stellar Solheim Cup career on top of her individual successes. She represented Europe eight times, is the second-highest points winner in history with 24 and was the Europe captain in 2017. What a career!

Annika continued to play until 2008 before deciding to move away from competitive golf. Annika has remained very busy since her retirement. She has developed her brand ANNIKA, alongside working as a golf course architect on many different projects. Annika married her second husband Mike McGee in 2009 and the pair have two children together.

She also recently returned to competitive golf when she stormed to an eight-shot victory at the US Senior Women's Open in 2021, with her husband as her caddie. Class really is permanent!

Sörenstam is thought by most to be the greatest women's golfer in recent history and has a trophy cabinet as big as anyone's on here. Is she the greatest LPGA player ever? That's for you to decide! But no list of the greatest golfers would be complete without Annika's name.

# TOM WATSON

## MAJORS

THE OPEN
CHAMPIONSHIP
X5

PGA
CHAMPIONSHIP
X0

US OPEN
X1

THE MASTERS
X2

**TOTAL MAJORS**
**8**

## CAREER STATS

| | |
|---|---|
| YEARS RANKED NO. 1 | 5 |
| PROFESSIONAL WINS | 70 |
| PGA TOUR WINS | 39 |
| EUROPEAN TOUR WINS | 8 |
| RYDER CUP RECORD | 10–4–1 |
| PGA TOUR CHAMPIONS WINS | 14 |

| PGA WIN % | PRIZE MONEY |
|---|---|
| 39/619 (6.3%) | $11,081,140 |

Ryder Cup record is in the format of wins-losses-halves

# BIOGRAPHY

| | |
|---|---|
| BORN | SEPTEMBER 4, 1949 |
| NATIONALITY | AMERICAN |
| TURNED PRO | 1971 |
| HEIGHT | 1.75 M (5 FT 9 IN) |
| PLAYS | RIGHT-HANDED |

Tom Watson is a true champion of the game and is still one of the most famous names in golf today. He won eight majors, including an incredible five titles at the Open, won 39 PGA Tour events, and is a Ryder Cup legend as both a player and captain.

Watson was a consistent player throughout his career, but had an eight year period of sheer brilliance from 1977-1984. During this time, he was named PGA Player of the Year six times (including four in a row from 1977-1980, won the Vardon Trophy three consecutive years from 1977-1979, and had many epic battles with Jack Nicklaus, often coming out on top against golf's greatest-ever major winner.

Thomas Sturges Watson was born in Kansas City, Missouri, in September 1949. Tom's father Ray was a fan of golf and bought his son golf lessons at a young age at the Kansas City Country Club. As is so often the case, Tom's talent was immediate to see, and by the time Tom had started high school, he was already known to be a great golfer in his local area.

Tom continued to develop his game throughout his teenage years and had his first taste of real success at the age of 17 when he won the Missouri State Amateur championships, which was a feat that he repeated three more times in the next four years. Tom's impressive results as a junior got the attention of many universities across America, and the future star eventually joined Stanford in 1969 to study psychology. Watson impressed during his three years of university, and his performances were good enough to gain him entry into his first major at the 1970 Masters. Watson failed to make the cut this time, but as we all know, he would be back many times in the future and it would not be long until he was wearing the green jacket.

Watson graduated from Stanford in 1971 and joined the PGA Tour shortly after. He spent his first few years adjusting to life as a professional and working on his game. By the time it was 1974, he had improved greatly as a player and was ready to show the world that he could mix it with the best.

Watson's previous best result at a major was a 29th-placed finish in 1972 before coming into the 1974 US Open, but no one would have guessed this when the young American held the 54-hole lead by one stroke. It was all a bit too much too soon for Tom and he capitulated in the fourth round, shooting 79 to finish fifth, but his golf over the first three days had still impressed the world.

It wasn't just the fans who had been wowed: following the final round, golfing legend Byron Nelson (who we will cover later on) approached Tom and offered to coach him. Byron liked Tom's playing style but could see he needed some help to become the great player we know today. The pair started working together a few months later and Tom credits much of his future success to the help that Byron gave him.

Tom was clearly very upset after his collapse at the 1974 US Open, but rather than let this result get him down for long, he did what true champions do and bounced straight back. Only two weeks later, he came from six shots behind on the final day to win the Western Open! This win proved his talent and shut down any doubts that he couldn't handle the pressure, which was a much needed confidence boost for Tom.

Tom's rise to the top of the game from this point on was unstoppable. He entered his first Open Championship in 1975 but seemed like a seasoned pro when he won his first major in dramatic fashion. Tom sunk a 20-foot putt for birdie on the 18th hole of the final day to force a playoff with Jack Newton, before beating him by one stroke in the 18-hole playoff to win the first of his five Open titles.

As you will remember from the introduction to this biography, the period soon after this first major was one of complete dominance from Watson. From 1977 to 1983 he won seven more majors, including two at the Masters in 1977 and 1981, one at the US Open in 1982, and five in nine years at the Open. Remember, this was a time when legendary players such as Jack Nicklaus and Seve Ballesteros were at the peak of their powers, which made this run of form from Watson even more impressive.

Perhaps Tom's greatest performance over his whole career came at the 1977 Open when he had one of golf's most epic duels with none other than Jack Nicklaus. He and Jack started off solidly, both shooting 68 and 70 in the opening two rounds to finish in a tie for second on two-under. The two were paired together for the third round, but they could once again not be separated after becoming run-away leaders with scores of 65.

The two were once again paired together on the final day and were tied going into the 17th. It was clear that playing 'par golf' was not going to be enough to get the win when these two legends were battling it out, and that someone would have to do something special to win. Watson birdied the 17th to go one up into the final hole, but Jack did not give up there. He holed a 40-foot putt on the 18th to bring the scores level, but incredibly this was not enough. Tom stuck his approach to two feet from the hole for a tap-in birdie on the last to finish on 12-under par, one ahead of Jack Nicklaus and 11 strokes ahead of third place. What a rivalry!

Despite Tom's dominance over this period, he was never able to win the PGA Championships and complete the career grand slam. He came top 10 in the event ten times and came as close as one can be in 1978 when he came second but unfortunately, it was not meant to be.

Watson won his final PGA Tour event in 1998 but continued to compete in majors until 2009. Not only did he compete, but he went on one of the most remarkable major runs in history at the 2009 Open. Watson was 59 years old and had been ruled out as a contender for many years, but he rolled back the years and showed that no matter what age he was, he was there to win. In perhaps the biggest shock in golf history, Watson held the lead going into the final hole of the last day. All he had to do was par the 18th and he would become a six-time Open winner and the oldest major winner in history by a long way. Sadly, Watson was unable to make par on the last and eventually lost in a four-hole playoff to Stewart Cink. Despite not quite getting the win, it is still one of the greatest major runs ever and is something that only a player as great as Tom Watson could achieve.

On top of these incredible individual performances, Watson also performed impressively at the Ryder Cup. He represented the USA four times, was on the winning side for three of those and won 10.5 points from a possible 15.

Watson achieved a period of dominance that has rarely been seen before in the golfing world. He was part of some of the most legendary tournament duels in history with Jack Nicklaus, often coming out on top, and was so good that he could still compete with the very best up to his late 50s. Players like him certainly don't come around often.

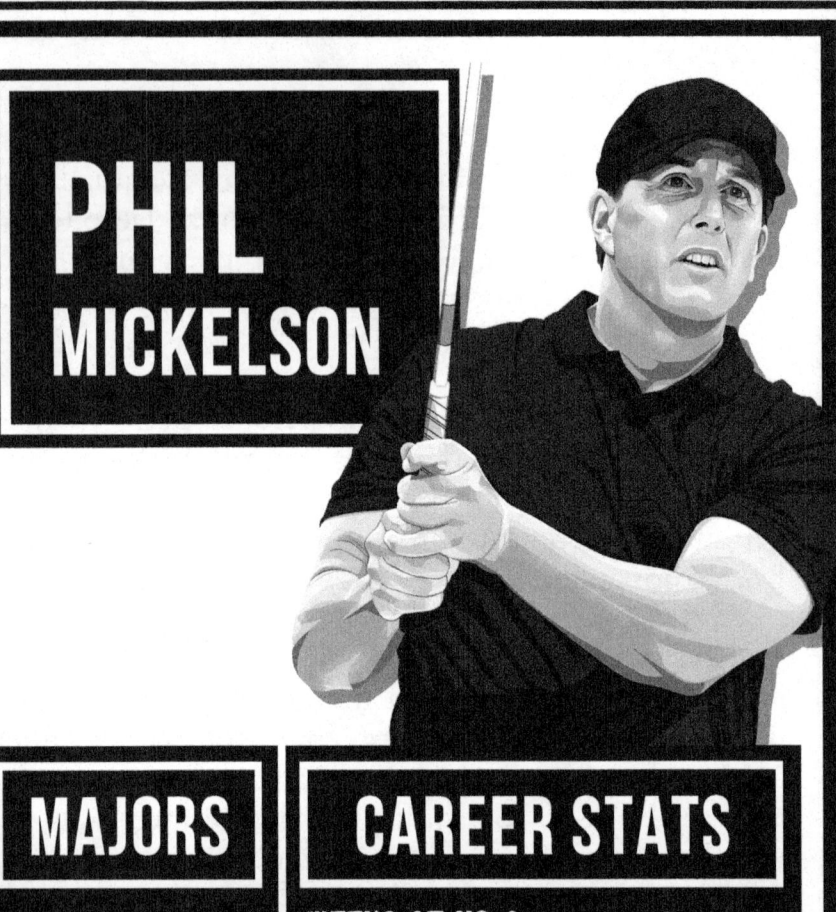

# PHIL
## MICKELSON

## MAJORS

THE OPEN
CHAMPIONSHIP
**X1**

PGA
CHAMPIONSHIP
**X2**

US OPEN
**X0**

THE MASTERS
**X3**

| TOTAL MAJORS |
| :---: |
| 6 |

## CAREER STATS

| | |
| :--- | :---: |
| WEEKS AT NO. 1 | 0 |
| PROFESSIONAL WINS | 57 |
| PGA TOUR WINS | 45 |
| EUROPEAN TOUR WINS | 11 |
| RYDER CUP RECORD | 18-22-7 |
| THE PLAYERS CHAMPIONSHIP | 1 |

| PGA WIN % | PRIZE MONEY |
| :---: | :---: |
| 45/662 (6.8%) | $96,572,310 |

| | |
|---|---|
| **BORN** | **JUNE 16, 1970** |
| **NATIONALITY** | **AMERICAN** |
| **TURNED PRO** | **1992** |
| **HEIGHT** | **1.91 M (6 FT 3 IN)** |
| **PLAYS** | **LEFT-HANDED** |

It seems only fitting that we follow up the oldest runner-up at a major with the oldest player in history to win a major championship - Phil Mickelson.

I'm sure that you are all familiar with the iconic (and at times controversial) golfer nicknamed 'Lefty'. Mickelson has been a hot topic with the media in recent years, ranging from his unbelievable victory at the 2021 PGA Championship to become the oldest major winner in history at the age of 50, to his questionable switch to LIV golf one year later.

But, like him or not, Mickelson is undoubtedly one of the greatest golfers of the last 30 years, and one of the greatest of all time for that matter. He is the winner of 45 PGA Tour events, six majors and has finished second in majors a further 12 times. Not only this, but at times he seemed to be the only person with a chance of dethroning Tiger in his prime, getting the better of him in some epic duels across the years.

Philip Alfred Mickelson was born in San Diego, California in June 1970. Phil's father (also called Phil) was an amateur golfer, and his uncle was a caddie at Pebble Beach, so Phil was exposed to the sport at a young age. It is said that he started taking his first shots at just 18 months old, and by the time he reached elementary school, his dad would take him out to their local course a few times a week.

Amazingly, the man nicknamed 'Lefty' is actually a natural right-hander. However, as a small child he learned by watching his father's swing (who was right-handed) front-on, and the mirror effect meant that the young Phil developed his left-handed swing by chance.

Phil practiced very hard as a junior, especially focussing on his short game that he would become so famous for as a pro in years to come, and the results started to show in junior tournaments. He won many junior tournaments in the San Diego area, and by the time he graduated high school, he had won three consecutive national Junior Player of the Year awards.

Mickelson's incredible results as a teenager meant that he had his pick of universities, and in 1989 he enrolled at Arizona State University. They had high hopes that Phil would bring them golf glory, and wow did he deliver. Mickelson won three NCAA individual championships whilst at university along with three Haskins Awards given to the best college golfer of the year.

Not only did Mickelson excel at college golf, but he was already making waves as an amateur on the PGA Tour. Phil was invited to play the 1990 US Open, where he finished a respectable 29th, before making the cut in all three of the majors that he played in the following year. If you thought those were impressive results for an amateur, then wait for this. He became just the seventh amateur in history at the time to win a PGA Tour event when he won the 1991 Northern Telecom Open by one stroke. Amazing!

It was clear that he was the best young golf prospect in

the country and big things were expected of him when he turned pro in 1992.

Mickelson took to professional life immediately, winning two more PGA events in his first year as a pro. From 1992-2003 Phil established himself as one of the best players on tour. He won 20 PGA Tour events, first moved into the top ten in the rankings in 1996, and first became world number two in 2001.

On a side note, Phil would go on to spend over 700 weeks in the top 10 in the world over his career, including 270 weeks ranked at number two, but unbelievably never made it to number one in the world. Tiger Woods was in his prime for much of this period, and no matter how many tournaments Phil won, there was no overtaking the great one. For context, the player with the second longest number of weeks at world number two never to make it to world number one is Jim Furyk with 39 weeks. Mickelson is definitely the greatest golfer ever never to get to that number one spot!

Although he was performing very well in PGA Tour events over these 11 years, he could not quite get over the line at the majors. In fact, Phil finished top three at a major eight times without getting a win. It seemed that although he was a great player, his game just wasn't quite there to win on the biggest stage.

This all changed in 2004 at one of the most exciting final days in Masters history. Mickelson held a tie for the lead with Chris DiMarco on six under aftcr the third round but it was Ernie Els that Mickelson battled it out with on day four. Els went out two groups ahead of Mickelson and shot a five-under 67 to finish on 8-under and pile the pressure on Phil. Mickelson shot an uninspiring 38 on the front 9 and coming into the final seven holes, needed five birdies to get the win. As had been the case so many times over the last decade, it seemed that Mickelson was going to come as close to winning as possible, before faltering at the last minute. But this tournament was different...

Mickelson birdied four of the next five holes and came into the 18th, tied with Els and knowing that a birdie would secure his first green jacket with no playoff needed. Mickelson played the final hole like a true champion, finding the green in two before sinking the 15-footer to win his first major in incredible style. After all those second and third places, he had finally gone one further and the floodgates were about to open.

Phil won the PGA Championships the following year and repeated his victory at the Masters in 2006, before winning the Masters again in 2010 and the Open Championship in 2013.

Perhaps the most memorable of these major wins was at the Open in 2013. Mickelson came into the final round in a tie for ninth place, five strokes behind leader Lee Westwood. Mickelson shot a staggering 66 on the final day in tough conditions where the rest of the field struggled, finishing as a relatively comfortable winner by three strokes on three-under-par. It was such a good round that Mickelson's caddy from 1992-2017 - Jim 'Bones' Mackay - said in an interview that it was the "best round of Phil's career".

Phil was 43 when he won the Open and many believed

that it would be his last. He continued to compete at the top of the game over the next eight years, finishing second in three more majors late into his forties, but it seemed that his days of winning majors were over. This could not have been more wrong.

Phil came into the 2021 PGA Championship as a 50-year-old on pretty poor form. No one even considered him as a contender for the title. In classic Mickelson style, he defied the odds and did the unthinkable. Mickelson led from round two onwards, holding off fightbacks from Koepka and Oosthuizen to win the tournament for a second time and become the oldest major winner in history. It was one of the greatest moments in golf history and shows never to write Phil off, no matter how old he is.

Unsurprisingly, Mickelson has been in the headlines many times since this win, both for good and for bad reasons. He was one of the first 'big name' golfers to join the new Saudi-backed LIV Golf as well as revealing that he had a serious gambling problem over the past three decades where he was rumoured to have wagered over $1 billion with over $100 million in losses. Whatever your opinions are on LIV Golf, we can all agree that gambling addiction is a serious problem, but thankfully Phil has received professional help for this and is recovering every day.

Despite having some bad press off the course, Phil's golf had the final word in 2023 when he rolled back the years once more to finish second at the Masters. Phil started the final day 10 strokes off the lead, but equalled the lowest score at the Masters for 27 years when he shot a final round 65 to finish runner-up behind Jon Rahm.

Phil has shown us time and time again that he is one of the greatest players ever to grace a golf course, and it would not be surprising at all if he had a few more deep runs, or even wins, in majors to come. Not only did Phil win six majors over his career, but he finished second a further 12 times, usually losing out to the sheer brilliance of Tiger Woods.

We can only imagine how many more majors Phil would have won and how long he would have been world number one had Tiger not been around.

# LEE TREVINO

## MAJORS

**THE OPEN CHAMPIONSHIP**
X2

**PGA CHAMPIONSHIP**
X2

**US OPEN**
X2

**THE MASTERS**
X0

**TOTAL MAJORS**
6

## CAREER STATS

| | |
|---|---|
| PROFESSIONAL WINS | 92 |
| PGA TOUR WINS | 29 |
| EUROPEAN TOUR WINS | 5 |
| RYDER CUP RECORD | 17-7-6 |
| PGA TOUR CHAMPIONS WINS | 29 |
| PGA PLAYER OF THE YEAR | 1 |

| PGA WIN % | PRIZE MONEY |
|---|---|
| 29/481 (6%) | $3,478,328 |

Ryder Cup record is in the format of wins-losses-halves

| BORN | DECEMBER 1, 1939 |
| --- | --- |
| NATIONALITY | AMERICAN |
| TURNED PRO | 1960 |
| HEIGHT | 1.70 M (5 FT 7 IN) |
| PLAYS | RIGHT-HANDED |

# BIOGRAPHY

Lee Trevino may not be one of the most well-known golfers on this list, but he was one of the most dominant golfers of his era, winning six majors and 29 PGA Tour events in his career, and his story is one of the most incredible. He was not only known for his brilliant golf, but also for his fantastic sense of humour, incredibly kind nature, and terrible bad luck with injuries.

When I say bad luck with injuries, I really mean it. Aside from suffering almost career-ending back injuries multiple times, he was struck by lightning while on the course in 1975 and still managed to come back and win another major. Truly incredible!

Lee Buck Trevino was born in December 1939 in Garland, Texas into a family of Mexican ancestry. Sadly Lee never knew his father, who left when he was small, and was raised by his mother and grandfather. Back in the day when Lee was born, golf was seen as a sport for the wealthy and many of the other golfers on this list, especially the older ones, had a very privileged upbringing. This was not the case for Lee and this makes his rise to the very top even more impressive.

Lee had to start working at the age of just five to earn money for his family. He started off working in the cotton fields which often got in the way of his schooling, but he always attended when he had the time. Lee has always been a real hustler, which was undoubtedly influenced by having to work and provide for his family at such a young age.

Luckily for the young Lee, his family home was very close to Dallas Athletic Golf Club. He was first introduced to golf by his uncle, who would give him a few golf balls and an old club to use after hours on the local course. Lee also realised that he could make a few extra bucks on the course and would go around finding old balls and reselling them to members.

By the time Lee was 14, he was obsessed with golf. He left school to become a full-time caddie and shoe shiner at his local club where he was paid $30 a week, but more importantly, this gave him access to three golf holes behind their shack. He reportedly hit 300 balls a day, many of which were off a very hard surface, which gave him the slightly unusual compact swing that he would later become famous for.

Lee worked and practised relentlessly until he enrolled in the United States Marine Corps in 1956 at 17. He served four years as a machine gunner but was able to practice and play golf very regularly, competing in many events across Asia during this time.

Following his discharge from the Marines, Lee turned professional, but it would take many years before he was regularly competing on the PGA Tour. As I mentioned earlier, Lee was a natural-born hustler, and he made a lot of his money over the next six years betting on himself in **head-to-head** matches against other golfers. Of course, Lee came out on top much more than he lost, and he was able to use this money to start travelling and playing in bigger tournaments.

It was not the standard route that legendary golfers took once they turned pro, but he would later credit this time to helping him deal with pressure in the biggest moments. There is a fantastic quote from later in Lee's career where he said "You don't know what pressure is, until you've played for five dollars a hole with two dollars in your pocket".

Lee's first taste of the big time came at the 1966 US Open, where he qualified for the first time and impressively made the cut.

Just one year later, he got the opportunity to play the US Open again and he took it with both arms wide open. The relatively unknown boy from Texas stunned the world by finishing fifth, which not only earned him $6,000 but showed himself and the world what he was capable of. He finished 1967 as Rookie of the Year and was ready to take his golf to the next level.

The following year Lee did the unthinkable. It was just his third appearance at the US Open and fourth appearance at a major in total, and Lee was yet to win on the PGA Tour, but he played like a seasoned pro. He comfortably won the tournament by four strokes over Jack Nicklaus, scoring under 70 in every round and showing nerves of steel throughout. Not only this, but he equalled the tournament scoring record! Lee's long and unlikely road to becoming a golf pro was complete - he had won the first of his six majors and beaten the best in the world to do so.

This win kickstarted a run of 14 consecutive years where Trevino won at least one tournament on the PGA Tour. Lee's second and third majors came in 1971 where he played arguably the best golf over a 20-day period in history. He started it by beating Jack Nicklaus in a nail-biting 18-hole playoff to win his second major at the US Open. He followed this up with the first of his three wins at the Canadian Open two weeks later, and if that wasn't impressive enough, he won the Open the following week.

This made him the first person in history to win these three events in one year and cemented his spot as the best golfer of the year.

Trevino defended his Open title the following year in one of the most clutch moments in major history. He birdied the final five holes, which included holing a bunker shot and chipping in from 30 yards, to beat Jack Nicklaus by one stroke again.

He then beat Nicklaus by one stroke once again two years later to win the first of his two PGA Championships. It is safe to say that all those money matches as a young adult made Trevino one of the best pressure players in the history of golf! By this point, he had won five majors and had never come second!

The next ten years were a time of terrible luck for Lee and a constant struggle for full fitness. He was struck by lightning at the Western Open in 1975 in a freak accident that is every golfer's worst nightmare. This caused him to suffer bad injuries to his spine which required surgery. Miraculously, despite still struggling with back issues, Trevino came back to the Tour and won at least one event for the next seven years following his injury.

By the time it was the 1984 PGA Championships, Trevino was 44 years old and had not won a tournament for three years. He was already a legend of course, but everyone had counted him out as a serious contender. As he did so many times in his career, Trevino defied the odds to win the tournament by four strokes with a score of 15-under par. Not only this, but he became the first player to shoot all four rounds under 70 at the PGA Championships.

This proved to be Trevino's last win on the PGA Tour but he wasn't finished setting records there. He switched to the Champions Tour at the age of 50 in 1989 and proved that his golfing class was permanent. He won 29 events including four senior majors, which puts him third in the all-time list of wins on the Champions Tour.

No matter where Lee played golf, whether it was for $5 at his local course as a 21-year-old, or at the age of 60 on the Champions Tour, he always gave it his all and was one of the fiercest opponents around every time.

Trevino will always be remembered for his incredible performances at the majors and, in particular, his nerves of steel and clutch comebacks when it really counted. He is one of the only players in history to consistently get the better of Jack Nicklaus, and he deserves his spot in this book just for that! What he is perhaps best known for is his hilarious sense of humour and very kind and giving nature.

# WALTER HAGEN

## MAJORS

THE OPEN
CHAMPIONSHIP
**X4**

PGA
CHAMPIONSHIP
**X5**

US OPEN
**X2**

THE MASTERS
**X0**

| TOTAL MAJORS |
|:---:|
| 11 |

## CAREER STATS

| | |
|---|---|
| PROFESSIONAL WINS | 58 |
| PGA TOUR WINS | 45 |
| RYDER CUP RECORD | 7-1-1 |
| RYDER CUP WINS AS CAPTAIN | 4 |
| WORLD GOLF HALL OF FAME INDUCTION | 1974 |

| MAJORS TOP 5 | MAJORS CUTS |
|:---:|:---:|
| 25/57 (44%) | 51/57 (89%) |

Ryder Cup record is in the format of wins-losses-halves

# BIOGRAPHY

| | |
|---|---|
| BORN | DECEMBER 21, 1892 |
| NATIONALITY | AMERICAN |
| TURNED PRO | 1912 |
| HEIGHT | 1.79 M (5 FT 10 IN) |
| PLAYS | RIGHT-HANDED |

Walter Hagen is one of the oldest golfers on this list, being born a whopping 130 years ago, but his legend lives on just as strong. Hagen sits third on the all-time majors list, with 11 wins, and was the all-time leader from 1929 to 1972. What makes this even more impressive is that the Masters did not exist for the first 20 years of his career so he achieved all these wins with just three majors on offer.

Hagen was not only a legend on the course, but he was a true **trailblazer** off it. He was one of the most flamboyant and stylish golfers of his era and drew in crowds bigger than any other golfer before him. Hagen put golf on the map to millions of new fans worldwide, constantly fought to raise the conditions for pro golfers and is rumoured to be one of the first athletes in history to become a millionaire from sport. There is no doubt that golf today would not be the same without Walter Hagen.

Walter Charles Hagen was born in Rochester, New York, in December 1892 into a working-class family with German origins. He was the second of five children and the only boy.

Just as with Trevino, Hagen had to start earning money for his family at a young age, so he got a job as a caddie at Country Club of Rochester Golf Club at the age of nine. The young Walter received a meagre 10 cents per round (equivalent to about $4 today) plus some small tips, but it did give him access to the course during off-peak hours.

Hagen played golf at every opportunity possible, which was noticed by the head pro Alfred Ricketts who started helping the young man with his game. By the time Walter was in his mid-teens, he was one of the best players at the club. This didn't go unnoticed and he was asked to start coaching and work in the pro shop.

Hagen continued to develop his game at any opportunity possible, and by the time he was 19, he made his pro debut at the Canadian Open. Walter was still in his teens, and completely unknown at this point, so little was expected of him, but he surprised everyone to finish in a respectable 11th place.

Just one year later in 1913, Walter had earned the right to play in his first major at the US Open. This had seemed like an impossible dream for Walter, but through his hard work and perseverance, he had made it happen. However, his admission to the tournament was not well respected by the other golfers who didn't know who he was, and he later said that "they pushed him off the tee and told him he could practice when they were through". Many would have felt intimidated by comments like these, but not Walter Hagen. This only motivated him to do better and he shocked everyone by finishing in a tie for fourth.

The golf world would have to get used to Walter Hagen's golf shocking them as it would happen countless times in the future. Still angered by the disrespect his fellow golfers had shown him, Walter vowed to play in the US Open the following year and win it. Well, guess what? He did exactly that.

Hagen held off a tough challenge from amateur Chick Evans to win the tournament by one stroke on two-over-par and took home $300 for his efforts. That's the equivalent of Hagen caddying for 3000 rounds when he was younger!

World War 1 broke out around this time, causing many golf tournaments to be cancelled, so Hagen had to wait until 1919 to win his second major. During this time, Hagen also became the first golfer in the world to be a touring professional not to be associated with a club. A true trailblazer!

The period of 1919-1929 was one of the most dominant golf has ever seen. Walter won ten majors, consisting of five PGA Championships (including four in a row from 1924-1927), four Open Championships and one more US Open. What made this stretch even more impressive was that he had to compete against the first big wave of very talented golfers such as Bobby Jones and Gene Sarazen (both of whom we will cover later).

Hagen was never able to get the better of Jones in majors when they both competed, but he did beat him in a world-famous 72-hole exhibition match in 1926.

Hagen's game was never considered to be as polished as these two, but as truly great players do, he always found a way to win at the crucial moments. Hagen perhaps hit more erratic drives and approaches than any other player on this list, but his **recovery game** was just so good that he almost always got away with it.

He was also one of the first golfers to train his psychology, which is something he often used to his advantage. Golf was regularly a match-play format back then and Hagen was known for using some very sneaky tricks to win. He was known to select **woods** from short distances to trick his opponent into thinking they had a further distance from the hole. Of course, Hagen knew that this was the wrong club choice so he would **choke down** on it, but his opponent would copy his choice of club and send it flying over the green. While the sportsmanship is perhaps a little questionable, you can't deny that it is quite brilliant.

As we said in the introduction, Hagen also improved the standards of golf pros greatly during this time. Back then, as crazy as it seems, it was looked down upon to earn money from sport and play it professionally. Clubs would often not even let pro golfers into the clubhouse at tournaments! In fact, at the 1920 Open, Hagen was once again not allowed to enter the clubhouse, so he instead rented a limousine with a chauffeur which he parked directly in front of the clubhouse and used as his own personal dressing room. It was stunts like this that helped to change how professionals were treated and he played a key role in forming the Professional Golfers Association of America - the PGA - in 1916.

Hagen's legendary golf status doesn't stop there. He played a vital role in the early days of the Ryder Cup and was the US captain for the first six editions of the competition from 1927-1937. He captained the US to four wins out of six and was the first captain to win on English soil.

Walter Hagen truly is one of the all-time greats who perhaps had a bigger impact on the sport than anyone else in history.

A quote by fellow legend Gene Sarazen sums his legacy up perfectly - "All the professionals ... should say a silent thanks to Walter Hagen each time they stretch a check between their fingers. It was Walter who made professional golf what it is."

A real legend of the game.

# MICKEY WRIGHT

## MAJORS

WESTERN OPEN
**X3**

TITLEHOLDERS
CHAMPIONSHIP
**X2**

CHEVRON
CHAMPIONSHIP
**X0**

WOMEN'S PGA
CHAMPIONSHIP
**X4**

US WOMEN'S OPEN
**X4**

**TOTAL MAJORS**
**13**

## CAREER STATS

| | |
|---|---|
| PROFESSIONAL WINS | 90 |
| LPGA TOUR WINS | 82 |
| LPGA TOUR MONEY WINNER | 4 |
| LPGA VARE TROPHY | 5 |
| WORLD GOLF HALL OF FAME INDUCTION | 1976 |
| BOB JONES AWARD | 1 |
| ASSOCIATED PRESS FEMALE ATHLETE OF THE YEAR | 2 |

| BORN | FEBRUARY 14, 1935 |
|---|---|
| NATIONALITY | AMERICAN |
| TURNED PRO | 1954 |
| HEIGHT | 1.75 M (5 FT 9 IN) |
| PLAYS | RIGHT-HANDED |

# BIOGRAPHY

It would be tough for anyone to follow a golfer with the calibre and impact on the game as Walter Hagen did, but if anyone was going to do it, it would be Mickey Wright.

Mickey is considered by many to be one of the greatest LPGA Tour players of all time and she definitely has the accolades to back that up. Wright is a 13-time major winner which puts her second in the all-time list, and what makes this even more impressive is that she won these over only eight years. She is second on the all-time LPGA Tour winners list with 82 tournament wins, she won the Vare Trophy on five different occasions and comfortably holds the record for most LPGA Tour events won in a single year with 13 wins in 1963!

Not only was she a serial winner, but she also had a near-flawless swing and was capable of regularly bombing her drives over 300 yards. Players like Mickey Wright don't come around often!

Mary Kathryn Wright was born in February 1935 in San Diego, California. She started playing golf at 12 and showed an immediate talent for the sport. She had a glittering junior career, winning many prestigious tournaments while still in her teens. The highlights of these were the 1952 US Girls Junior and the 1954 World Amateur Championship among many others.

Mickey's talents and potential were clear for all to see and it came as no surprise to anyone that she went on to be one of the greatest players in history.

Her amazing golf ability was spotted by many universities across America and she attended Stanford University at the age of 18 where she studied psychology and was their star player. Wright had a very successful time at Stanford, but it was clear after a few years that she was ready to take the next step in her golf career. She finished as the low amateur at the 1954 US Women's Open and shortly after decided that it was the right time to turn pro.

She joined the LPGA Tour in 1955 and it didn't take her long to start beating the very best.

Mickey won her first tournament in 1956 at the Jacksonville Open, which started a streak of 14 consecutive years where she would win at least one LPGA Tour event. She won her first major at the 1958 LPGA Championship, breezing to a six-stroke victory, which started a seven-year period where she won at least one major each year.

Mickey was incredibly dominant on tour throughout her career, but over the years of 1961-1964, she was on another level. She won 10 LPGA Tour events in 1961 and 1962, 13 in 1963 and 11 in 1964, which included eight majors. Only four other golfers in history have won in the double-digits in a single season of the LPGA Tour and Mickey did it for four consecutive years. Unsurprisingly, she topped the LPGA Tour money list and won the LPGA Vare Trophy for each of these years. Unstoppable!

In 1964, at the Tall City Open, Wright completed perhaps the greatest final-round comeback that the LPGA Tour has ever seen. She shot a 62 to come back from ten shots back to win the title. Not only was this the lowest LPGA Tour round in history at the time (and four strokes better than the best men's round on this course), but it was also the largest final-round comeback in the history of the LPGA Tour, which is a record that she still shares with none other than Annika Sörenstam.

Mickey's 13th and last major win came at the 1966 Women's Western Open. She continued to perform very well on the LPGA Tour for the next three years, winning many more tournaments, before she was eventually forced to retire from full-time golf at 34 in 1969 because of problems with her feet and wrists.

She still played some events after this, even winning the 1973 Colgate-Dinah Shore Winner's Circle, but her time at the top of the game was over. She made her final LPGA Tour appearance in 1980 and officially retired from competitive golf in 1995, although she continued to hit 40-50 balls every day long after her retirement.

Choosing the greatest LPGA Tour player of all time is a tricky thing to do and is completely up to you, but there is no denying that Mickey Wright deserves to be near the top of anyone's list. She had one of the nicest swings in history, broke almost every record under the sun and had a four year period of dominance that may never be seen again in the history of golf. She is one of golf's greatest champions who will never be forgotten.

# JACK
## NICKLAUS

## MAJORS

THE OPEN
CHAMPIONSHIP
X3

PGA
CHAMPIONSHIP
X5

US OPEN
X4

THE MASTERS
X6

**TOTAL MAJORS**
**18**

## CAREER STATS

| | |
|---|---|
| YEARS AT NO. 1 | 10 |
| PROFESSIONAL WINS | 117 |
| PGA TOUR WINS | 73 |
| EUROPEAN TOUR WINS | 9 |
| RYDER CUP RECORD | 17-8-3 |
| PGA PLAYER OF THE YEAR | 5 |

| PGA WIN % | PRIZE MONEY |
|---|---|
| 73/584 (12.5%) | $5,734,031 |

Ryder Cup record is in the format of wins-losses-halves

| BORN | JANUARY 21, 1940 |
|---|---|
| NATIONALITY | AMERICAN |
| TURNED PRO | 1961 |
| HEIGHT | 1.78 M (5 FT 10 IN) |
| PLAYS | RIGHT-HANDED |

# BIOGRAPHY

Now we move on to the man who has won the most golf major championships out of any player, man or woman, in the history of golf - Jack 'The Golden Bear' Nicklaus.

Nicklaus is three majors ahead of second-placed Tiger Woods and Patty Berg with 18 wins to his name. He holds the record for most wins at the Masters with 6, is the joint record holder at both the PGA Championship and the US Open with five and four wins respectively and won a further three times at the Open. He is third on the all-time PGA winners list with 73 wins and was named the PGA Player of the Year five times throughout his incredible career.

Not only did he dominate golf to such a great extent, but he consistently did so for such a long time, having a 24-year gap between his first and last major wins. Jack Nicklaus truly is a once-in-a-lifetime talent, who will go down in golf history as perhaps the greatest champion ever.

Jack was born in January 1940, in Columbus, Ohio into a family of German descent. His father Charlie was a very talented athlete who played semi-pro football (American football), was a local tennis champion and also played golf off a scratch handicap so Jack was set up to be a top athlete from birth.

Jack competed in many different sports as a child and was especially talented as a shooting guard in basketball, but golf was his true passion throughout. He started playing at the age of 10 at the Scioto Country Club and was hooked straight away.

He soon started getting coaching from the club pro Jack Grout and the two gelled well together. In fact, Grout was Jack's coach throughout his entire career so he certainly got lucky to find him at such a young age.

As you would expect, it did not take Jack long to become one of the most feared junior golfers in the country. He won the first of his five consecutive Ohio State Junior Titles at 12. By the time he was 13, he had shot his first round under 70, become the years youngest qualifier for the US Junior Amateur and had a handicap of +3.

Jack's junior career only got better and better, and by the time he was 17, he had already won 27 events in the Ohio area. Jack's impressive results as a teenager gave him his first chance to compete in a major which he did at the 1957 US Open. Although he didn't make the cut this year, he returned even stronger in 1958 and made the cut, finishing in a tie for 41st.

Despite now regularly competing on the PGA Tour, Nicklaus decided to attend Ohio State University from 1957-1961 to study pharmacy like his father had done. During his time there he won almost everything that college golf had to offer. He won the US Amateur twice in 1959 and 1961 and the NCAA Championship in 1961, but it wasn't just in college golf that he was making a name for himself. He came second at the 1960 US

Open, finishing two strokes behind champion Arnold Palmer, and set the amateur-record score of 282.

Despite his young age of 21, Jack had already had one of the most successful amateur careers in golf history and, in November 1961, he turned pro.

It only took Jack two majors as a pro until he got his first win. Arnold Palmer led Jack almost throughout the 1962 US Open, but in true champion style, Nicklaus performed best when it mattered the most and finished the final round in a share of the lead with Palmer on one-under-par. Despite the crowd being against the youngster, Jack held off a spirited fightback by Palmer to win the 18-hole playoff by three strokes and become the youngest US Open winner since Bobby Jones in 1923. Nicklaus had announced himself to the world and it was now not a question of if he would win another major, but when and how many.

The wait for Nicklaus' next major win was a very short one and he won both the Masters and the PGA Championship in 1963.

Nicklaus won two more Masters titles in the following three years before completing the career Grand Slam at the Open in 1966. This made him the fifth man in history to achieve this, but little did anyone know that he would complete the career Grand Slam three times over his career.

By the time it was 1972, Nicklaus had tied Walter Hagen's majors record with 11 and needed just one more to be the all-time leader. As expected, it took him just one more year to break this record, which he did when he won the 1973 PGA Championship. This made him the greatest champion in the history of men's major golf tournaments, but as we all know, he did not stop there.

From 1974-1980, Jack won a further five majors which brought his total up to 17. This period also included his worst year on tour. In 1979, he suffered a bad dip in form and didn't win an event on the PGA Tour for the first time in his career as a professional. As he did so many times, however, Nicklaus silenced the critics the following year by winning both the US Open and the PGA Championship.

Jack was now in his forties and it seemed that he was past his best. Over the next five years, he continued to compete at the very highest level, getting three second-placed finishes at majors, but couldn't add to his tally.

Nicklaus was 46 years old when the 1986 Masters came around, and despite being a five-time champion, almost everyone had written him off as a genuine contender due to his age. The previous oldest winner at the Masters was Sam Snead at 41 years old, so it seemed almost impossible for Nicklaus to win another green jacket.

After the first three rounds, it seemed that this would be the case. Nicklaus came into the final round in a tie for ninth place on two-under-par and was four strokes back of 54-hole leader Greg Norman and three back from fellow legend Seve Ballesteros.

The final round of the 1986 Masters was one of the

most incredible and unforgettable rounds in golf history. Five different players held the lead over the course of the day and Nicklaus held the solo lead for the first time in the tournament on the 17th hole of the final day! After the 8th, Jack was six strokes back from Ballesteros and five back from Norman, but then he went on one of the most legendary **charges** in history. The 46-year-old made 6 birdies and an **eagle** over the final ten holes, shooting 30 on the back nine and 65 over the final 18, to win the tournament by one stroke. It would be considered one of the greatest Masters comebacks in history regardless of his age, but to do this at 46 is simply beyond belief.

Nicklaus continued to compete on a limited schedule on the PGA Tour up to the age of 65 in 2005! He started his very successful Senior PGA Tour career in 1990. The Golden Bear won eight senior major championships from 1990-1996 which puts him third on the all-time list.

Nicklaus was also a key member of the US Ryder Cup team throughout his career. He competed in six Ryder Cups from 1969-1981, winning five times and earning 18.5 points and was also the US captain in 1983 and 1987. Some critics have said that Jack slightly underperformed in the Ryder Cup, but this just shows the incredibly high standards that he set on an individual level. After all, he is the seventh-highest points winner for the United States and won twice as many matches as he lost.

This brings a close to the biography of the greatest major champion in the history of golf. Jack Nicklaus' career truly was one-of-a-kind. He never had the most technically perfect swings, was the cleanest ball striker or had the best all-round short game, but he found a way to win week-in week-out and that's what true champions do. They find ways to win even if their game isn't feeling 100% and always perform when the pressure is on in the biggest moments.

Jack Nicklaus' record of 18 major wins has stood strong for 38 years now. Do you think anyone will ever overtake him?

# BYRON NELSON

## MAJORS

THE OPEN
CHAMPIONSHIP
X0

PGA
CHAMPIONSHIP
X2

US OPEN
X1

THE MASTERS
X2

TOTAL MAJORS
5

## CAREER STATS

| | |
|---|---|
| PROFESSIONAL WINS | 64 |
| PGA TOUR WINS | 52 |
| VARDON TROPHY | 1 |
| PGA TOUR LEADING MONEY WINNER | 2 |
| WORLD GOLF HALL OF FAME INDUCTION | 1974 |

| PGA WIN % | PRIZE MONEY |
|---|---|
| 52/287 (18%) | $190,256 |

# BIOGRAPHY

| | |
|---|---|
| BORN | FEBRUARY 4, 1912 |
| NATIONALITY | AMERICAN |
| TURNED PRO | 1932 |
| HEIGHT | 1.85 M (6 FT 1 IN) |
| PLAYS | RIGHT-HANDED |

Byron Nelson was born well over 100 years ago but he is still one of the most well-known names in golf, and rightly so. He won a massive 52 times on the PGA Tour, putting him sixth on the all-time list, won five majors and won the Vardon Trophy in 1939. What makes these stats even more impressive is that World War II struck at the peak of his career, so we can only imagine how many more tournaments he would have won if this were not the case.

He was known for his fluid swing and almost mechanic-like irons that were deadly accurate, even winning the 1939 Western Open without leaving the fairway for the entire 72 holes. If that stat sounds ridiculous, then just wait until this one. He had the single greatest run of form in the history of golf in 1945 when he won 11 consecutive PGA Tour events, which is a record that has not come close to being beaten ever since and finished that year with a record 18 PGA Tour victories. When Byron was on form, no one even came close.

John Byron Nelson Jr. was born in February 1912 in Waxahachie, Texas, and was coincidentally born within seven months of fellow legendary champions and future rivals Ben Hogan and Sam Snead. He grew up in a Baptist household with parents who were very committed to their religion and helped out at his parent's church long after he became famous.

He moved to Fort Worth at the age of 11 and started caddying soon after at the Glen Garden Country Club, which is when he became friends with Ben Hogan who also happened to be a caddy at the club.

However, tragedy almost struck the young Byron before he was introduced to golf. He contracted typhoid fever in his first year in Fort Worth where he lost half his body weight and barely survived. How lucky the golf world is today that he was able to overcome this terrible disease and find his true passion shortly after.

Nelson knew nothing about golf before he started caddying but he learned very quickly and was soon practicing every day. Nelson and Hogan would compete against each other many times as professionals in the future but their first competitive match came in an annual caddy tournament at 14. Nelson won the nine-hole playoff by one stroke over his friend and their lifelong rivalry had begun.

Nelson continued to practice and improve his game relentlessly before turning pro at 20 in 1932.

The early 1930s were a very tough time in America and they were in a period known as the Great Depression. Money was very tight for the young Byron so he took a job as a club professional in Texas and played as many pro events as his budget could afford.

There was also a monumental change in golf technology happening in the 1930s. Until this point, golfers used wooden shafted clubs known as hickory golf clubs, but steel shafts had just been created and the top players were starting to switch over.

Nelson realised that changing shafts would change the limits of how the golf club could be swung and spent the first few years of his life as a professional adapting his swing. He was one of the first players to develop a full swing with greater leg drive in the downswing like we see today, which has since earned him the historic nickname of the father of the modern golf swing.

These tweaks and changes to his swing helped Byron to improve massively over the first three years of being a pro, and by the time it was 1935, he was ready to show the world how good he was.

He won his first PGA Tour event at the 1935 New Jersey State Open by three strokes and it seemed that all his hard work was paying off. Despite this win, he had still not earned much money from golf and was living paycheck to paycheck. He reportedly had just $5 to his name when he won his second PGA Tour event at the Metropolitan Open in 1936, but these financial troubles would all change the following year.

Nelson played one of the greatest rounds in Masters history en route to winning the tournament in 1937 for the first of his five major wins. He started the tournament with a record-breaking six-under 66, which stood as the lowest round at Augusta until 1976. He won the tournament by two strokes on five-under-par and collected the winner's check of $1500 (worth about $33,000 today).

This started a period of nine years where Nelson was undoubtedly the best golfer on the planet and few could touch him. He won the Masters again in 1942, won the US Open in 1939 and won the PGA Championship in 1940 and 1945.

Unfortunately for Byron, World War II broke out when he was at the peak of his career, meaning that many tournaments and majors were cancelled. In fact, 14 majors were cancelled from 1940-1945, so there is almost no doubt that he would have added to his tally if this was not the case.

Nelson was not conscripted to fight in the war like many others at this time because he had a blood disorder, but he used his golf skills to help the war effort. He gave hundreds of golf exhibitions across the country, each time raising significant amounts of money for charity, and was able to do more for the war than most from the comforts of the golf course.

1945 soon rolled around and Nelson was about to have perhaps the single greatest year in the history of golf (yes I've said this a lot, but this time I mean it). As we said earlier, he won a ridiculous 11 consecutive tournaments and finished the year winning 18 of the 30 events he played. These are records that no one has even come close to in the nearly 80 years since! Some critics of Nelson have tried to take away from the impressiveness of these results by saying that many of the top golfers were not competing in 1945 due to the war, but this was generally not true. The majority of the top golfers in the world, including Ben Hogan and Sam Snead, played an almost complete schedule that year and none could do anything to stop the sheer dominance of Byron.

Byron had had the greatest season in the history of golf and seemed to be in the peak of his career, but the strains of playing and travelling so much were taking its toll on the 34-year-old and he was getting tired of golf. To everyone's shock, he announced his retirement in 1946 and bought a ranch in Roanoke, Texas.

He did continue to compete on the PGA Tour, but never played a full schedule again. Despite this, he won six times on the PGA Tour in 1946 (not bad for someone who is technically 'retired') but only won once more after that. His rivals Sam Snead and Ben Hogan carried on playing for decades after Byron retired and won many more majors, so we can only imagine how many more majors Byron would have won if he hadn't retired so early.

Nelson remained active in the golf world after his retirement. He was a golf commentator in the 1960s and 70s and mentored some great players such as Tom Watson. In 1968 he became the first person to have a regularly-held PGA Tour event be named after a player when the Dallas Open was changed to the Byron Nelson Golf Classic.

Nelson met his first wife Louise in 1934, and the two were happily married until she passed away in 1985. He then met his second wife Peggy in 1986 and the two remained married until Byron passed away in 2006 at the impressive age of 94.

Byron Nelson was a real legend of the game who deserves all the recognition that he gets. Not only did he have perhaps the greatest year in golf history, but he was also a pioneer of the modern golf swing and one of the most accurate players of all time.

He may have won fewer majors than many others on this list, but he would have almost certainly won many more had it not been for World War II or his early retirement, and how we view him in terms of being one of the greatest ever needs to take this into account.

# PATTY BERG

## MAJORS

TITLEHOLDERS
CHAMPIONSHIP
**X7**

WOMEN'S PGA
CHAMPIONSHIP
**X0**

WESTERN OPEN
**X7**

US WOMEN'S OPEN
**X1**

TOTAL MAJORS
**15**

## CAREER STATS

| | |
|---|---|
| PROFESSIONAL WINS | 63 |
| LPGA TOUR WINS | 60 |
| WORLD GOLF HALL OF FAME INDUCTION | 1951 |
| LPGA TOUR MONEY WINNER | 3 |
| LPGA VARE TROPHY | 3 |
| BOB JONES AWARD | 1 |
| PATTY BERG AWARD | 1 |

BIOGRAPHY

| BORN | FEBRUARY 13, 1918 |
| NATIONALITY | AMERICAN |
| TURNED PRO | 1940 |
| HEIGHT | 1.57 M (5 FT 2 IN) |
| PLAYS | RIGHT-HANDED |

There are few players in the history of golf that can claim to have had as big of an impact on the world of golf as Patty Berg did. Not only is she the all-time leader in women's major championships with 15 wins, but she was also one of the founding members and the first president of the LPGA.

But wait, she's not done being a trailblazer there. Berg was one of the four original inductees into the LPGA Hall of Fame in 1951, was the second woman inducted into the PGA Hall of Fame in 1978, and has the Patty Berg Award named after her for outstanding contributions to women's golf (which she won in 1990).

Patty was not only one of the greatest champions in the history of golf, but she was a true pioneer of women's golf who laid the foundations for the prominence and popularity of it today.

Patricia Jane Berg was born in Minneapolis, Minnesota, in February 1918. Patty's first sporting love was surprisingly not golf, but rather, football (American football). As a child, she played as the quarterback for her local team and was even coached by future hall-of-famer Bud Wilkinson. Luckily for us all, she started playing golf at 13 and showed an immediate talent for the sport.

Just three years later at the age of 16, she won her first

big amateur title at the Minneapolis City Championship and the following year she won a state amateur title.

Patty attended the University of Minnesota at 17 which is where her results really took off. The teenager came in a shock second place at the US Women's Amateur and suddenly the whole world was aware of what she was capable of.

Two years later, in 1937, the Titleholders Championship was taking place for the first time and Patty had the chance to play and test herself against the very best. Patty came into the third and final round eight strokes behind the leader Helen Hicks, but in an incredible final-day comeback, she shot six-under to win the title by three strokes. Despite competing in her first-ever major and still being a teenager, Patty had done the impossible and won.

Berg defended her title at the Titleholders Championship and seemed completely unstoppable. However, just as we have seen with many other golfers on this list, World War II broke out which majorly disrupted her golf schedule and meant that she missed many chances to win more tournaments.

Despite this disruption, Patty turned pro in 1940 after winning a staggering 29 amateur titles. She signed a sponsorship deal with Wilson Sporting Goods which helped her greatly to fund the rest of her golfing career. From 1940-1945 Berg was only able to compete in three tournaments that would soon be recognised as majors, which were all at the Women's Western Open, and unsurprisingly won two of the three.

Patty's career almost came to a devastating end in this period as well when she was in a bad car crash in 1941 that shattered her knee. Many feared that this would be the end of her golf career, but she bravely came back to the sport in 1943 and was soon back to her very best. Not only did she return to golf after her injury but she also volunteered for the United States Marine Corps in 1942 and served in the Marine Reserves from 1942-1945. What a woman!

The war ended in 1945 which finally meant that Berg could play a full golf schedule and return all her attention to the course. She was an incredibly dominant force over the next 13 years and formed fierce rivalries with fellow all-time legends Louise Suggs and Babe Zaharias. Patty added ten more majors to her tally during this time, and the trio won 27 of the 42 majors on offer.

She did not just perform well in majors but was a consistent winner all year round. She won the LPGA Vare Trophy three times in 1953, 1955, and 1956 and was the LPGA Tour Money Winner in 1954, 1955, and 1957.

Although Patty often got the better of her rivals, we can only wonder how many more majors Patty would have won had she not been competing against some of the other greatest LPGA Tour players in history at the time.

Whilst she was busy winning tournaments on the course, she was also busy bringing about much-needed change for women's golf off it. She was one of the 13 founders of the LPGA Tour and served as its first president in 1950.

Her last win on the LPGA Tour came in 1962 but she continued to compete until the age of 62 in 1980 until a hip surgery forced her to permanently step away from the big tournaments.

Berg constantly helped others with their golf game throughout her career. It is said that she led more than 10,000 golf clinics in her life and continued running these all around the world into her old age.

The Patty Berg Award was established by the LPGA in 1978 and is awarded to 'the lady golfer who has made the greatest contribution to women's golf during the year'. It is a true testament to the contributions that Patty made to the LPGA over her career and immortalises Patty Berg's name in the LPGA Tour forever.

A true hero of women's golf and one of the greatest champions of all time. Is she the best ever? That part is up to you...

# ARNOLD PALMER

## MAJORS

THE OPEN
CHAMPIONSHIP
**X2**

PGA
CHAMPIONSHIP
**X0**

US OPEN
**X1**

THE MASTERS
**X4**

| TOTAL MAJORS |
|:---:|
| 7 |

## CAREER STATS

| | |
|---|---|
| PROFESSIONAL WINS | 95 |
| PGA TOUR WINS | 62 |
| EUROPEAN TOUR WINS | 2 |
| RYDER CUP RECORD | 22-8-2 |
| PGA TOUR CHAMPIONS WINS | 10 |
| VARDON TROPHY | 4 |

| PGA WIN % | PRIZE MONEY |
|:---:|:---:|
| 62/703 (8.8%) | $1,861,857 |

Ryder Cup record is in the format of wins-losses-halves

| BORN | SEPTEMBER 10, 1929 |
|---|---|
| NATIONALITY | AMERICAN |
| TURNED PRO | 1954 |
| HEIGHT | 1.78 M (5 FT 10 IN) |
| PLAYS | RIGHT-HANDED |

Arnold Palmer was one of the most popular and liked golfers of all time who even had a group of devout followers called 'Arnie's Army' who cheered him on wherever he played. He had an unorthodox swing which made him stand out among some of the other top golfers at the time, but he let his stellar results and countless records do the talking.

He was the first player to win the Masters four times, the first player to earn over $1 million in tournament prize money *and* won 62 times on the PGA Tour, putting him in fifth place all-time. It is rare that players can be both so liked by the crowds and so good at golf, but Palmer was a master at both.

Arnold Daniel Palmer was born in September 1929 in Latrobe, Pennsylvania into a working-class steel mill town. Arnold's father was a head pro and **greenskeeper** at Latrobe Country Club so he was introduced to golf right from birth. His father started him playing golf in his early years, and through much hard work and practice, he grew to be the top junior golfer in his area.

He won five West Penn Amateur Championships while still in his teens before attending Wake Forest College on a golf scholarship.

Now here is where his story is different from the

others. Arnold's close friend tragically lost his life in his early days at college, which affected Arnold greatly, causing him to leave college and enlist in the US Coast Guard for three years where he was barely able to play golf.

After his enlistment ended he returned to golf and it was not long until he was back to winning ways. He won the 1954 US Amateur and decided to turn pro later that year.

Palmer started life on the PGA Tour strong and only got better as the years went by. In his first year as a rookie, he won the first of his 62 PGA Tour events at the Canadian Open and recorded his first top-ten finish at the Masters. He then won two PGA events the following year in 1956 and followed this up with four wins in 1957. Palmer had now established himself as one of the best players in the world, but he was yet to finish in the top five of a major and some questions were being asked.

This would all change in 1958 and Palmer was about to start a run of seven magical years where he was almost unstoppable. Palmer and Sam Snead came into the final round of the 1958 Masters in a tie for the lead, but the 45-year-old Snead could not keep up with Arnold, who won the tournament by one stroke on four-under-par.

Palmer may have been a somewhat surprise winner at the time, but the Masters crowd would get very used to seeing him wearing the green jacket in the years to come.

He won seven majors from 1958-1964, which included four wins at the Masters, two at the Open and one at the US Open and he finished in the top five in 17 of the 25 majors over this period. What made this even more impressive is that he was competing against some of the greatest golfers in history such as Gary Player or a young Jack Nicklaus.

Many of these wins were dramatic, tense and very memorable, but two stand out above the rest. We'll start with his win at the 1960 US Open, which was magical for so many reasons. Golf was at a crossroads at this moment. Ben Hogan was in the declining part of his career, Jack Nicklaus was just emerging as a top amateur and then there were Gary Player and Arnold Palmer who were just coming into the peaks of their careers.

After the third round, Hogan and Nicklaus were in a tie for fifth, Player was still in with a shot in tenth, and Palmer seemed way out of contention sat seven back in 15th. As you may have guessed, Palmer staged the single greatest comeback in US Open history and came back to win by two strokes over Jack Nicklaus. Palmer unbelievably birdied six of the first seven holes to card a 65 and come from behind to beat all of these great champions. Coming back from seven strokes behind in the final round of a major is incredible on its own, but to do it against so many great champions is simply unheard of.

Perhaps Palmer's other most memorable win was at the 1962 Masters where he won the third of his four green jackets. Palmer was leading by two after the third round, but after a poor final round of 75 where he made two clutch birdies on the 16th and 17th to stay in contention, he found himself in the first-ever three-way tie in Masters history with Gary Player and Dow Finsterwald. Palmer showed nerves of steel to card a 68 in the 18-hole playoff, beating Player by three strokes and Finsterwald by nine.

Palmer remained a regular winner on Tour over the next seven years, but could not add to his seven majors. He recorded five second-placed finishes at majors in this period and his last big year on Tour was in 1971 when he won four events.

Palmer was an integral part of the US Ryder Cup team throughout the 60s and early 70s and finished his career with one of the greatest Ryder Cup records of all time. He won 23 points out of 32 matches for the US team and his 22 victories mean he has the most of any American player in history. Palmer also had two stints as Ryder Cup captain where he was equally successful. He captained the US team in 1963 and 1975 where they won by 14 and 10 points respectively.

Palmer continued to play excellent golf as he grew older and joined the Champions Tour in 1980. Palmer's likeable and charismatic character caused a surge in popularity for the new tour, and many have questioned whether it would have had the success that it does today if it weren't for Palmer joining at the start. Palmer went on to win five senior majors between 1980 and 1985, even winning his last one at the Senior Players Championship by 11 strokes.

Arnold was a very successful businessman off the course and was regularly amongst the highest annual earners for athletes well into his 80s. His business empire included course management companies, clothing lines, golf channels, golf academies and many more. He certainly stayed busy in his retirement!

Palmer passed away in 2016 at the age of 87, but his legacy lives on forever. He will always be remembered for his charismatic personality, unique swing and for being one of the greatest champions in the history of golf.

# BOBBY JONES

## MAJORS

**THE OPEN CHAMPIONSHIP**
X3

**US AMATEUR**
X5

**BRITISH AMATEUR**
X1

**US OPEN**
X4

**THE MASTERS**
X0

**TOTAL MAJORS**
13

## CAREER STATS

| | |
|---|---|
| PROFESSIONAL WINS | 9 |
| PGA TOUR WINS | 9 |
| GRAND SLAMS | 1 |
| WORLD GOLF HALL OF FAME INDUCTION | 1974 |
| JAMES E. SULLIVAN AWARD | 1 |

| MAJORS TOP 5 | MAJORS TOP 25 |
|---|---|
| 25/43 (58%) | 33/43 (77%) |

# BIOGRAPHY

| BORN | MARCH 17, 1902 |
|---|---|
| NATIONALITY | AMERICAN |
| TURNED PRO | 1930 |
| HEIGHT | 1.73 M (5 FT 8 IN) |
| PLAYS | RIGHT-HANDED |

Bobby Jones' legacy in golf is perhaps greater than any other player in the history of the game. This is a man who won golf's first-ever Grand Slam, helped design Augusta National Golf Club and founded the Masters! It doesn't get better than that.

He won a staggering 13 majors (including the US Amateur and the British Amateur) despite stopping competing seriously when he was only 28 to focus on his family and career as a lawyer, so we can only imagine how many more he would have won had he played as long as the others in this book.

Jones was not only known for being a natural champion on the course but also a true gentleman. Despite his fame and success, he always played with integrity, class, and incredible respect for the game. Jones regularly reminded fans that some things were more important than winning and was even known to call penalties on himself that cost him major championships. His golf morals were so strong that he never even turned pro, meaning that he didn't earn any prize money over his career. A real legend in every way who is without doubt the greatest amateur in the history of golf.

Robert Tyre 'Bobby' Jones, Jr. was born in March 1902 in Atlanta, Georgia. He suffered from many health problems as a young boy and was prescribed to play golf in order to strengthen him up (that's more fun than taking some medicine right?). He started golf at a very young age and fell in love with it immediately. He won his first tournament at six and shot his first round of 70 at 12.

By the time he was 14, Bobby was able to drive the ball a whopping 250 yards. You have to remember that this was in 1916 so he was using clubs with a wooden shaft and rubber balls. Imagine how far he could have hit it with today's technology. This sheer power helped him to win the Georgia Amateur Championship that same year, beating adults twice his age, and put his name in the national spotlight for the first time. It also automatically qualified him to play in his first major at the US Amateur, where he made it to the quarter-finals. Imagine finishing in the final eight of your first major at just 14 years old!

Jones was called golf's next prodigy after these incredible results and the pressure got to him over the next few years. His results did not match his expectations and he failed to win anything bigger than some regional events over the rest of his teens.

However, he was still improving and performing consistently even if he wasn't winning. He played in his first US Open at 18 in 1920, finishing in 8th, and played his first Open a year later in 1921.

You will remember how much praise we gave Jones' character in the introduction, and he truly deserves it, but in his teenage years this was not the case. He was actually known as a bit of a hothead back then, and perhaps his worst moment came at this first Open

Championship in 1921. He picked up his ball halfway through the third round and walked off because he was frustrated that he couldn't get out of a bunker.

At this point in his career, it seemed that Jones was just another talented golfer who couldn't handle the pressure and would never challenge for golf's biggest titles, but this would soon all change. In 1922, at the age of 20, he went through a total transformation and became the respectful and disciplined gentleman that we all know him to be today and the golf results soon followed.

Jones finished in second at the 1922 US Open, before getting his hands on the first of his 13 majors at the same tournament the year after, but it wasn't without drama. Jones came into the 72nd hole three strokes ahead of Bobby Cruickshank in second place, and it seemed that Jones would cruise to his first major win. However, to the surprise of everyone watching, Jones made a double bogey and his opponent birdied the last so the two went to an 18-hole-playoff. Luckily, Jones didn't live to regret this blowup and beat Cruickshank by two strokes in the playoff to win the title.

This started a period of eight years of incredible golf where Jones could not stop winning tournaments. From 1923-1930 Jones won 13 of the 21 majors he played and only didn't finish in the top two four times.

The highlight of the golden period was of course 1930 when he became the first person in history to win the original Grand Slam consisting of The Open, the US Open, the US Amateur and the British Amateur. What made this even more impressive is that Jones called this result before the first tournament of the year was played. He placed a bet on himself to win all four majors at odds of 50-1 at the start of the year and collected $60,000 for his winnings. Now, we don't recommend gambling at any time, but you have to admire his confidence and belief in his game!

As we mentioned earlier, Jones remained an amateur throughout his entire time as a golfer, and a big reason for that was that he always focused on his education, career, and family, no matter how many tournaments he was winning.

He graduated from the Georgia Institute of Technology in 1922 with a degree in engineering and then received another degree at Harvard in English literature two years later. In 1926 he enroled in Emory University's law programme and passed the Georgia **bar exam** after just three semesters and began practising law at his father's company in 1928.

He married Mary Malone in 1924 and the pair had three children together. How he had any time to play golf, let alone be the greatest player on the planet, is amazing.

Either way, after winning the Grand Slam in 1930, Jones felt that he had achieved what he wanted in golf and retired, now focussing on spending time with his family and law firm.

Despite no longer playing regularly on Tour, he still remained very active in the world of golf. Jones filmed many instructional videos and wrote multiple books about golf, but by far his most impressive achievement was helping create Augusta National Golf Club and setting up the Masters. The first Masters was played in 1934 and Jones played in every one until 1948. He was past his best at this point but still had multiple top-20 finishes.

Sadly Jones was diagnosed with a rare disease called **syringomyelia** in 1948 and could no longer play any golf after this. He took his final trip to the Masters in 1968 before passing away from this disease in 1971 at the age of 69.

Bobby Jones had one of the most incredible and unique careers in the history of golf. It is mind-blowing that he was able to achieve two degrees, become a lawyer, spend time with his wife and kids and still be one of the greatest golf champions ever. He showed that no matter how important your passion seems, always make time for your family and education and that is something we can all learn from.

# BABE
## ZAHARIAS

## MAJORS

**TITLEHOLDERS CHAMPIONSHIP**
X3

**US WOMEN'S OPEN**
X3

**WESTERN OPEN**
X4

**TOTAL MAJORS**
10

## CAREER STATS

| | |
|---|---|
| PROFESSIONAL WINS | 48 |
| LPGA TOUR WINS | 41 |
| WORLD GOLF HALL OF FAME INDUCTION | 1974 |
| LPGA TOUR MONEY WINNER | 2 |
| LPGA VARE TROPHY | 1 |
| BOB JONES AWARD | 1 |
| ATHLETICS OLYMPIC GOLD MEDALS | 2 |

| BORN | JUNE 26, 1911 |
|---|---|
| NATIONALITY | AMERICAN |
| TURNED PRO | 1947 |
| HEIGHT | 1.70 M (5 FT 7 IN) |
| PLAYS | RIGHT-HANDED |

Now we move on to Babe Didrikson Zaharias, and if you don't know anything about her or her career, then prepare to have your mind completely blown. We are not just talking about one of the greatest golfers ever to play the game (which she was of course), but perhaps the most well-rounded athlete, male or female, in the history of humanity.

She won ten majors, putting her in a tie for fourth place with Annika Sörenstam in the all-time list, won 41 times on the LPGA Tour, and completed the calendar Grand Slam in 1950 when she won all three majors on offer. She created history in 1938 when she became the first woman to compete in a men's event, and was one of the 13 founders of the LPGA Tour. A truly remarkable golfer!

Of course, we will be focussing on her golf career throughout this biography and it would take a whole book dedicated to her if we covered her whole life story, but we couldn't live with ourselves if we didn't at least list off some of the other ridiculous achievements that she had throughout her life. And by the way, she started exclusively playing golf at the age of 23, so all of these achievements were before then. So here goes...

**Track and Field** - She won three Olympic medals, all at the 1932 Olympics. She won gold in the 80m hurdles and javelin and silver in the high jump. Both gold medals were new world records. She is also the only athlete in history to win Olympic medals in separate jumping, throwing and running events.

**Baseball** - She got the nickname Babe (after Babe Ruth) when she hit five home runs in a single childhood baseball game. Later in life, she pitched four innings in three Major League Baseball exhibition games.

**Basketball** - She was the star of her work team, leading them to the AAU Basketball Championship in 1931. Not only this, but she was on the women's All-America basketball team from 1930-1932.

**Sewing** - She even competed in sewing competitions, once winning the South Texas State Fair competition, and made many of her golfing outfits.

**Music** - She was also a singer and harmonica player and recorded multiple songs with the major record label Mercury Records.

Phew... Now that we've got that out the way, we can finally start talking about what we're all here for - her golf career.

'Babe' Didrikson Zaharias was born in June 1911 and was the sixth of seven children to parents who immigrated to the US from Norway. Times were tough and money was tight for the family, so Babe and her siblings had multiple part-time jobs when they were young to help the family get by. Babe's mother was a great skier and skater and her father was a keen bodybuilder, so Babe was introduced to sports at a very young age.

Babe took to sports immediately and was a very competitive child, always wanting to beat the boys at whatever she did. As we have discussed earlier, Babe became world-class in multiple different sports and could be in an all-time legends book for many of these. By the time she started playing golf at the age of 21 in 1932, she was already a two-time Olympic gold medalist, had set multiple world records and had achieved more than most people could ever dream of. But of course, she was only just getting started...

Unsurprisingly to anyone, Babe was a natural at golf and it did not take long until she was beating players who had been playing their whole lives. It has been reported that in just her 11th round ever, she hit her first drive 260 yards, with wooden shafts and a rubber ball of course, and played the second nine with a score of 43.

She entered her first tournament in 1934, where she qualified with a score of 77, and after just two years of playing, she was close to being able to compete with the very best.

In a strange turn of events, she was forced to turn professional in 1935 after she accepted sponsorship money for her golf which meant that she was not allowed to compete in many tournaments. She spent the next few years travelling the country giving golf exhibitions, and perfecting her game.

She made history in 1938 when she became the first woman to compete in a PGA Tour event at the Los

Angeles Open. She did not make the cut this time, but this wasn't the last time she competed against the men. She played in three PGA Tour events in 1945 and defied all expectations by making the cut in two of these, showing that she could not only compete against the men but beat them. As of 2024, she is still the only woman in the history of golf to make the cut in a PGA Tour event, and she did twice!

Anyway, back to her rise to the top. Although still technically a professional, she was allowed to compete in the 1940 Women's Western Open and Babe did not let the opportunity slip. She cruised to her first major title, beating Mrs. Russell Mann in the final match 5 & 4. The woman who had already achieved so much in sport had reached the very top of yet another, but there was much more to come.

She regained her amateur status in 1942, meaning that she was free to compete in as many tournaments as she wanted, which sparked a period of true dominance for Babe and made her America's first female golf celebrity.

From 1944-1954 she won nine more majors and set record after record. In total, she won four Women's Western Open titles, three at the Titleholders Championship and three at the US Women's Open. She won a ridiculous 17 consecutive titles in 1947 which is still a record for an amateur golfer today, which included the British Ladies Amateur where she became the first American winner in history.

The rules about professionals playing in women's tournaments had changed by this point, so Babe turned professional for a second time in 1947 and was finally able to earn money for the incredible golf that she was playing. It wasn't long until she was the top money winner on Tour!

Babe's greatest year came in 1950 (yes, even better than 1947 when she won 17 straight events). She won the calendar Grand Slam and no one even came close to her. She won the Titleholders Championship by eight strokes, the Women's Western Open 5 & 3 in the final match and the US Women's Open by nine strokes. What made 1950 even more special is that she helped found the Ladies Professional Golf Association this same year, and was its star player alongside Patty Berg and Louise Suggs. It is undoubtedly one of the greatest years in the history of golf!

Babe's final major win came at the US Women's Open in 1954, and she won her final LPGA Tour event the following year at 44. She also served as the second president of the LPGA Tour during this time, doing so from 1952-1955.

Tragically Babe was diagnosed with colon cancer in 1953, and despite having successful surgery that year and making an incredible comeback to the Tour, the cancer returned in 1955 and she lost her life just one year later. Even in her times of great struggle at the end, she remained a fighter. She became a huge public advocate for cancer awareness and used her fame to receive massive donations to the American Cancer Society.

Babe Didrikson Zaharias' story is like no other. What she achieved throughout her life seems almost superhuman, and she will live on in the record books as not only one of the greatest golfers in history but perhaps the greatest all-around athlete of all time.

We can all take inspiration and motivation from her life. She never took no for an answer and always proved anyone wrong who doubted her through hard work and determination.

# GENE
## SARAZEN

## MAJORS

THE OPEN
CHAMPIONSHIP
**X1**

PGA
CHAMPIONSHIP
**X3**

US OPEN
**X2**

THE MASTERS
**X1**

| TOTAL MAJORS |
|:---:|
| 7 |

## CAREER STATS

| | |
|---|---|
| PROFESSIONAL WINS | 48 |
| PGA TOUR WINS | 38 |
| RYDER CUP RECORD | 7-2-3 |
| WORLD GOLF HALL OF FAME INDUCTION | 1974 |
| BOB JONES AWARD | 1 |
| SENIOR WINS | 3 |

| PGA WIN % | PRIZE MONEY |
|:---:|:---:|
| 38/316 (12%) | $76,815 |

# BIOGRAPHY

| | |
|---|---|
| BORN | FEBRUARY 27, 1902 |
| NATIONALITY | AMERICAN |
| TURNED PRO | 1920 |
| HEIGHT | 1.66 M (5 FT 6 IN) |
| PLAYS | RIGHT-HANDED |

Now we move on to Gene Sarazen who was the first person in history to win the modern career Grand Slam, won seven majors and played golf until he was 97! He also hit one of the most iconic and important shots in the history of golf, which you'll find about later on.

He was not only responsible for creating history on the course but also for changing how people played for years in the future. Sarazen is credited with creating the modern sand wedge, which helped people's games so much that courses were forced to change their designs to achieve the previous level of difficulty for the golfers. It is safe to say that Gene Sarazen left his mark on the world of golf.

Eugenio Saraceni was born in February 1902 in Harrison, New York. His parents were both immigrants from Sicily and money was tight for the Italian Americans. He started caddying at Larchmont Country Club at the age of eight to earn some extra cash for the family and immediately fell in love with golf.

Gene taught himself how to play right from the start, and unbelievably stayed self-taught throughout much of his teenage years, making his rise to the top even more impressive. What made Gene even more unique as a young golfer was that he was using the

**interlocking** grip, which although seems common now, was very rare for players to use in the early 1900s.

Sarazen continued to improve his game throughout his teenage years, and it was soon clear that he was destined to be a golf professional. He dropped out of school and took some assistant pro jobs at different clubs in New York.

His first big break in a major tournament came in 1920 at the US Open. He qualified from sectionals after making a stunning **albatross** on the final day (it won't be the first time he does something like this), and finished in a respectable 30th place. The world had its first glimpse of the great talent of Gene Sarazen and it wouldn't be long until he was all everyone was talking about.

It only took two more attempts until Sarazen got the first of his two wins at the US Open. He came into the tournament on good form, but legends such as Walter Hagen were still expected to be too good for the young man to beat. However, as he would do many times over his career, Gene defied the odds to win the title by one stroke. He fired an impressive final round 68 to come from four strokes behind on the final day to beat Bobby Jones by one and Walter Hagen by three. The young man who had to get a job caddying at the age of eight to earn money, and who taught himself the game of golf, had won the biggest tournament that golf had to offer, and he was not done there.

Sarazen put aside any doubts that this was a fluke by winning the PGA Championship just one month later and incredibly defended his PGA Championship title the following year. The young man had now won three of the first seven majors he had played in, and it seemed he was on track to be one of the greatest golfers in history. This would happen of course, but not quite in the timeline that you might expect.

Sarazen continued to perform well over the next nine years, and won multiple important tournaments, but could not add to his majors tally of three. He had six top-three finishes at majors over this period, but it seemed that his killer instinct when it really mattered had left him.

Gene struggled particularly with his sand play over these years. He partly blamed this on the old style of wedges used to play bunkers, so set about making his own club with a completely different design which he called the sand iron. This new club proved revolutionary and completely changed how bunker shots were played. Previously, players had **hit the ball clean** out of bunkers, but Gene's new club allowed for a completely different technique. Gene started contacting the sand a few inches behind the ball, giving him much more control over his bunker play, and this is a technique that all top players have used ever since. A true pioneer!

Anyway, Gene first started using this new sand wedge in 1932, and this just happened to be the year when he started winning again. Is this a coincidence? I think not.

Sarazen returned to winning ways at the Open Championship that same year, storming to victory and shutting down anyone who thought that he was not good enough to win another major. He led the Open from **wire-to-wire**, cruising to a five-stroke victory, finishing at five-under-par.

He followed this up with his second win at the US Open just a few weeks later and won his third PGA Championship and sixth career major the following year. Gene Sarazen was back on top of the golfing world and was achieving all the success that his hard work deserved.

The early 1930s were a special time in the world of golf, and the most iconic tournament in golf history was first starting - the Masters. Gene had already won the three other majors, so victory at the Masters would mean that he had won them all and would be the first person ever to complete the modern career Grand Slam.

He was unable to play in the very first Masters in 1934, but he more than made up for it the following year and was part of one of the most special moments in Masters history.

Gene was playing well heading into the final round and was three strokes off the lead on four-under-par. But when he was still three strokes behind on the 15th on the final day, it seemed his chances at a first Masters win were all but over. This was until Gene hit a shot on the par five 15th that became known as the "shot heard 'round the world." In truly unbelievable scenes, Gene holed his four wood from 235 yards out to make an albatross and get him in a tie for the lead. The timing and skill of this shot was simply so ridiculous and it is rightly still remembered as one of the all-time greatest shots in Masters history. The bridge approaching the 15th green was even renamed the Sarazen Bridge in 1955 to mark the 20th anniversary of this legendary albatross.

This was enough to get him into an 18-hole playoff with Craig Wood and Gene was not going to let this opportunity slip. He won the playoff by five strokes, and from that day on became the first person in history to win all four of golf's modern majors. What a legend!

Sarazen continued to perform well at majors over the later years of his career but could not add to his total of seven. His final win on the PGA Tour came in 1941 but he remained active in the golf world for the rest of his life.

He played at the Masters almost every year from 1935-1973, often hitting the ceremonial first tee shot alongside many other legends covered in this book. He was presented with almost every award that golf has to offer in his older years before eventually passing away at the very old age of 97 in 1999.

Sarazen had one of the most incredible careers out of anyone in the history of golf. He faced tremendous success at such a young age, and then recovered from a career slump to win four more majors and hit perhaps the greatest shot in golf history. A true legend who lives on forever in golf history.

# BEN HOGAN

## MAJORS

THE OPEN
CHAMPIONSHIP
**X1**

PGA
CHAMPIONSHIP
**X2**

US OPEN
**X4**

THE MASTERS
**X2**

**TOTAL MAJORS
9**

## CAREER STATS

| | |
|---|---|
| PROFESSIONAL WINS | 71 |
| PGA TOUR WINS | 64 |
| RYDER CUP RECORD | 3-0-0 |
| PGA TOUR LEADING MONEY WINNER | 5 |
| PGA PLAYER OF THE YEAR | 4 |
| VARDON TROPHY | 3 |

| PGA WIN % 64/300 (21%) | PRIZE MONEY $332,516 |
|---|---|

Ryder Cup record is in the format of wins-losses-halves

# BIOGRAPHY

| | |
|---|---|
| BORN | AUGUST 13, 1912 |
| NATIONALITY | AMERICAN |
| TURNED PRO | 1930 |
| HEIGHT | 1.74 M (5 FT 9 IN) |
| PLAYS | RIGHT-HANDED |

Ben Hogan may be last on this list but he is without doubt one of the greatest champions in the history of golf who had one of the toughest but most inspiring careers. He won nine majors, won 64 times on the PGA Tour and became the second player behind Gene Sarazen to win the modern career Grand Slam in 1953.

What makes these wins even more incredible is that Hogan had a terrible car crash in 1949 where doctors feared that he may never walk again. Hogan proved everyone wrong and came back and had the best years of his career, winning many more majors and proving that you could never count him out. What a true inspiration.

Hogan was also famous for being one of the hardest working golfers in history, who practised day and night on his swing and was also one of the first players to attach **yardages** to all his clubs. This hard practice not only made him one of the greatest winners on Tour, but also one of the most consistent. He finished in the top three in 47.6% of the 292 PGA Tour events he played and it is no wonder that he won the Vardon Trophy three times.

William Ben Hogan was born in Stephenville, Texas in August 1912 and was the youngest child of parents Chester and Clara. Life was not easy for the Hogan's growing up and they faced the worst tragedy imaginable when Ben was only nine. His father had been in a dark place for a while and tragically took his own life. Losing his father had a huge impact on Ben, and it caused him to become very **introverted**, which is how he remained for the rest of his life.

This loss also had bad effects on the family's finances and all the siblings were forced to take up jobs. Ben's first job was as a newspaper delivery boy, but luckily for the whole world of golf, Ben's friend recommended he start caddying at his local club at the age of 11 and that is where he was first introduced to golf.

He got a job at Glen Garden Country Club which just happened to be the same club that a young Byron Nelson was caddying at and the two soon became friends. Hogan took to golf immediately and practised hard whenever he had the opportunity. He did not have the chance to compete in many tournaments away from his local club, but he did have good local competition. Byron Nelson famously got the better of Hogan in a caddy tournament at the age of 14 after a playoff, but Ben would get the better of him many times later in their career as their rivalry developed.

Ben had known for a long time already that his career was going to be in golf, so he dropped out of school in the final semester of his senior year and turned pro at 17 in 1930. He spent the first few years playing pro events in Texas, but he was battling with a bad **hook** and wasn't getting the results he was hoping for.

Through some incredibly hard practising and his amazing work ethic, Ben was able to change his swing throughout the 30s, and by the time it was 1938 he was playing with the light fade that he would play with for the rest of his career. This more reliable shot shape made his game much more solid and consistent and the results soon followed. He won his first PGA Tour event in 1938, as well as making his first appearance at the Masters where he finished 25th.

As we have read many times before, World War II caused him to miss many events, although he was still able to compete in smaller PGA Tour events and racked up an impressive 20 Tour victories from 1940-1945. Hogan had established himself as one of the most solid players on Tour, but he was now well into his thirties and had not won a major, so it looked like time was slipping away.

However, Ben Hogan had other ideas and his career was only getting started.

Hogan's first full year back on tour was incredible. He won 13 times on the PGA Tour and this finally included what he had come so close to before - his first major win. He comfortably beat Ed Oliver 6&4 to win the PGA Championship and it was the start of eight years of stunning golf from Ben.

He won his second and third majors in 1948 at the US Open and the PGA Championship which earned him the first of his four PGA Tour Player of the Year awards. He was on top of the golf world at this point, but it all almost came crashing down in 1949.

Hogan and his wife were involved in a terrible crash with a bus, where they both almost lost their lives.

Hogan heroically flung himself over his wife in order to protect her, and this incredibly brave move likely saved both their lives. Hogan's bravery had saved them, but it left him with terrible injuries. He had broken four different bones and suffered a near-deadly blood clot and doctors told him that he would be lucky to walk again, let alone play golf.

As we have read many times in this biography already, Hogan never let others tell him that he couldn't do something, and worked tirelessly to regain his strength enough to get back to the PGA Tour. He was back playing eight months after the crash and miraculously was ready for the start of the 1950 season.

Hogan did the unthinkable at the 1950 US Open, which has gone down in history as one of the greatest comebacks in golf history. Despite being in severe pain due to his injuries, Hogan edged out a tight three-way playoff to win the tournament just over a year after his near-fatal crash. It was such an incredible win that it has since been called the 'Miracle at Merion'.

Hogan's injuries meant he couldn't play a full schedule for the rest of his career, but against all odds, he started playing the best golf of his life and no one could come close to him in the majors.

Hogan won five majors over the next three years and had one of the best seasons in history in 1953. He won his second Masters title, his fourth US Open title and his first Open Championship, and could only not compete in the PGA Championship due to scheduling problems. This win at the Open meant he had won the career Grand Slam, and also made him the first player in history to win these three majors in the same year. It also meant that he had won nine of the last 16 majors he had played. Unstoppable!

These proved to be Hogan's last major wins and his career slowly started to wind down. He had a few more second-placed finishes at majors in the following years, but his injuries and age were catching up to him. Hogan's final win on the PGA Tour came in 1959 and he played in his final Masters in 1967, finishing in a very respectable 10th place.

Hogan remained active in the golf world throughout his retirement. He wrote multiple golf books, teaching people about the secrets of his swing that he mastered over thousands of hours of practice and set up a successful clothing company before passing away in 1997 at the age of 84.

Hogan's story is one of the most incredible and inspiring of any golfer on this list. He faced so many tragedies and yet was always able to come back better and stronger through hard work and determination. He is a true inspiration and role model to us all.

# THE 19TH HOLE

You've made it to the end! You've learned all about the 20 greatest golfers and how each one changed golf history in their own way.

You can now choose your own greatest player of all time and I am sure that many of yours will be different. They may not even be on this list and that is completely fine! Whoever you choose, I hope that they inspire you and give you the motivation to go out and play and practice, and be the best golfer that you can be. I certainly know it does for me!

But most importantly, I hope that this list shows you that truly anyone can make it to the very top of golf. Yes, there are some players who had privileged upbringings with plenty of money, but there are also many players where this was not the case. These players overcame countless setbacks and hardships but through hard work, determination, and perseverance, made it to the very top in golf and wrote their names in the history books.

No one would have believed that Lee Trevino would be a six-time major winner after having to work on cotton fields as a five-year-old to earn extra money for his family, or that Seve Ballesteros would be the greatest champion in the history of the European Tour after building his own golf club as a child out of a wooden stick and a discarded club head. Yet, here they are, going down as some of the greatest champions that golf has ever seen.

These players prove that it doesn't matter where you're from, how many setbacks you face or how many people doubt you: anyone can become the very best in the world with dedication, passion and by never giving up on your dreams.

# GLOSSARY

**Albatross** – A score of three-under-par. It is sometimes also known as a double eagle.

**Apartheid** – A terrible system that existed in South Africa from 1948 until the early 1990s. Despite only making up 13% of the country, white people ruled South Africa and treated black people and other racial minorities like second-class citizens and enforced horrendous segregation and racism.

**Attach yardages** – To give distances to each club. I.e. this 9 iron goes 145 yards.

**Bar exam** – An exam that all lawyers need to pass.

**Birdie** – A score of one-under-par.

**Bogey** – A score of one-over-par.

**Caddie** – A person who helps a golfer on the course by carrying their clubs and giving them advice.

**Calendar Grand Slam** – Winning all majors on offer in a calendar year.

**Career Grand Slam** – Winning four majors over a player's career. For men, this means winning the Masters, the Open, the US Open and the PGA Championships. Women currently have five majors, but it is considered a career Grand Slam if they win four of these.

**Charge** – A stretch of holes where a player makes amazing scores, often to catch the leaders on the final day of a tournament.

**Chip-in** – When a player uses an iron to chip the ball in the hole from off the green.

**Choke down** – This means gripping lower on the club. It increases accuracy but decreases distance.

**Double bogey** – A score of two-over-par.

**Draw** – When the ball moves slightly right-to-left in the air.

**Eagle** – A score of two-under-par.

**Fade** – When the ball moves slightly left-to-right in the air.

**Green Jacket** – This is awarded to the winner of the Masters. It has been given to the winner since 1949.

**Greenskeeper** – A person who is responsible for looking after a golf course.

**Handicap** – This is a number that shows how many strokes a player is expected to play over par (or under par if you are a pro like these guys). If a person has a handicap of 15, they are expected to play an 18-hole round of golf with 15 shots over par.

**Head-to-head** – Two golfers who are competing against just each other.

**Hit the ball clean** – Hit the ball first without making contact with the ground before.

**Hook** - When the ball moves sharply from right-to-left in the air.

**Ignorance** – A lack of knowledge and understanding of a certain topic.

**Interlocking grip** – The most common golf grip used today. It is where the little finger and forefinger interlock with each other.

**Introvert** – A quiet and shy person.

**Majors** – The most important tournaments in men's and women's golf. For the men, these are the Masters, the Open, the US Open and the PGA Championships. For the women, these are the Chevron Championship, the Women's PGA Championship, the US Women's Open, the Amundi Evian Championship and the Women's Open.

**Make the cut** – Usually, just over half the players are 'cut' after the second round of a tournament. Making the cut means a player has scored well enough to carry on for the final two rounds.

**Match play** – A type of golf where players play directly against one opponent in a head-to-head match.

**Par** – The score that a very good golfer is expected to get on a hole.

**Par golf** – Playing steady and safe golf with the intent of just making pars.

**Playoff** – This is how a tournament is decided if two or more players are tied at the end.

**Prejudice** – An opinion a person already has without any actual reason or experience.

**Purse** – The total amount of money on offer as a prize.

**Recovery game** – Playing shots from tricky and often hazardous positions on the course to try to rescue the hole and make a good score.

**Re-mortgage** – To change your old mortgage with a new mortgage. It is often done to save money.

**Sportsmanship** – Playing sports in a fair and respectful way.

**Syringomyelia** – A dangerous disease that affects the spinal cord.

**Three-putt** – When a golfer needs three putts while on the green to get the ball in the hole.

**Tour card** – A player needs one of these to play on a specific pro tour. I.e. a player needs a PGA Tour card to play on the PGA Tour.

**Trailblazer** – A person who is the first to do something.

**Triple bogey** - A score of three-over-par.

**Up-and-down** – When a player is off the green, but is able to hit their shot onto the green and make the next putt.

**Wire-to-wire** – When a player has the lead for the whole tournament.

**Woods** – Clubs used to hit long shots.

Printed in Dunstable, United Kingdom